INFERNO

DANTE ALIGHIERI

Introduction and Notes by
John Lotherington

BARNES & NOBLE

NEW YORK

BARNES & NOBLE

NEW YORK

387 Park Avenue South
New York, NY 10016

Introduction, Endnotes, and Further Reading
© 2012 by Sterling Publishing Co., Inc.

This 2012 edition published by Sterling Publishing Co., Inc.

ISBN 978-1-4351-3658-8 (print format)
ISBN 978-1-4351-4113-1 (ebook)

For information about custom editions, special sales,
and premium and corporate purchases,
please contact Sterling Special Sales at 800-805-5489 or
specialsales@sterlingpublishing.com

Manufactured in the United States of America

2 4 6 8 10 9 7 5 3

www.sterlingpublishing.com

INFERNO

Contents

CANTO XX

CANTO XXI

CANTO XXII

CANTO XXIII

CANTO XXIV

CANTO XXV

CANTO XXVI

CANTO XXXIII

CANTO XXXIV

THE LIFE AND TIMES OF DANTE ALIGHIERI

Please note that many of the dates regarding Dante's writings are not known for certain and vary according to different sources.

1215   Faction fighting (which starts with a marriage dispute between two families) begins in Florence; it will continue into Dante's time, causing his exile and, then, the bitter reflection on disorder and treachery that runs through the *Inferno.* The initial divisions occur between Guelf families (who originally support the papal cause in the struggle for supreme authority) and Ghibellines (who originally support the imperial side). "Guelf" and "Ghibelline," however, end up serving more as banners for shifting factions and alliances than representing steady support for any papal or imperial cause.

1250   Emperor Frederick II—a regular point of reference in the *Inferno*—dies, adding further instability to Italy, which is already riven by conflict. He was crowned king of Sicily in 1198, at the age of three, and he accumulated other crowns and territory from then on, becoming Holy Roman emperor in 1220.

1260   The Battle of Montaperti, near Siena, sees the defeat of the Guelfs and the temporary triumph of the Ghibellines.

1265   Dante Alighieri is born in Florence. His parents will die in the 1270s, while he is still a boy.

1266   Beatrice Portinari, who will be Dante's great muse, is born in Florence.

1274   Dante and Beatrice first encounter one another.

1277   Dante's family promises him in marriage to Gemma di Manetto Donati, a member of a powerful Florentine family. (It is not known for certain when this betrothal became an actual marriage—probably in 1285.) The couple will have at least four children together.

1280   Dante begins composing his first sonnets on the theme of love.

1285   Dante fights as a member of the Florentine militia, seeking to take the castle of Poggio di Santa Cecilia back from the Ghibellines, who have raised a rebellion there.

1289   Dante again engages in military action—this time at the Battle of Campaldino, in the cavalry. His side (Florence and its Guelf allies) triumphs over the rival Ghibelline forces of Arezzo. Later in the year, he takes part in the siege and seizure of the fortress of Caprona.

1290   Beatrice Portinari dies at the age of twenty-four.

1293   Dante experiences a sublime sense of Beatrice in heaven and decides to study philosophy, rather than view everything poetic through the medium of love poetry as hitherto.

1295   By this year, Dante has finished *La vita nuova*, commentaries in Italian on his own poems from the previous decade or so, built on an autobiographical framework.

Dante enters political life in Florence. To do so, he joins the Guild of Physicians and Apothecaries (who also, fittingly, sell books), as a law has been passed during this year requiring that those who are going to hold office must first join a guild (as opposed to relying solely on noble connections). Within a few months, Dante will become a member of the Council of the Hundred, and part of the Consiglio dei Trentasei del Capitano (thirty-six representatives of the populace).

1300   The *Inferno*, *Purgatorio*, and *Paradiso* (which have not been written by this point) are set at Easter of this year. It is a year of pilgrimage and jubilee in Rome, as well as the year in which Dante turns thirty-five, "midway upon the journey" of his life.

Dante is elected one of the six ruling priors of Florence in June and holds office until August. During spring and summer, violence breaks out between the two factions into which the Guelfs have by now split: the Whites and the Blacks. Dante is among the White Guelfs.

1301   Dante is sent on a mission to Rome to negotiate with Pope Boniface VIII to ward off the threat posed by the forces of French prince Charles of Valois. However, the pope conspires with Charles and the Black Guelfs to overthrow the White Guelfs, and Dante is one of many who become exiles.

1302   Dante is formally banished from Florence under threat of death. An attempt by the White Guelfs to join forces with the Ghibelline exiles and retake Florence is abortive.

Dante begins *De vulgari eloquentia,* a Latin treatise defending the use of the vernacular; he will work on it until 1305.

1303   Pope Boniface VIII dies, having held his position since 1294. Though dead by the time the *Inferno* is written, he was alive during the period in which the epic takes place. In the work, he serves as an archetypically wicked pope, and there is a scene in which he is shown to be expected in Hell, where he will be plunged headfirst into the ground with his feet on fire.

1304   A final effort is made by the exiles to return in force to Florence, but this attempt also comes to nothing, and they fall apart in quarrels among themselves. Dante will spend the ensuing years at the courts of friendly rulers, primarily the della Scala family at Verona, and the da Polenta family at Ravenna.

Dante begins *Il convivio,* which he will complete in 1307. It is a "banquet" (the English translation of *convivio*) of ideas, written in Italian, in which he serves up philosophy, seeking to grasp the *intelligenze* (the intelligences that govern the heavens).

1307   In or around this year, Dante begins writing the *Inferno.*

1310   German king Henry VII (who will become Holy Roman emperor) enters Italy to impose his authority. It is Dante's greatest hope that this ruler will triumph and then restore peace to Italy.

1311   Dante attends the coronation of future emperor Henry VII as king of Italy, in Milan, and writes three public letters in support of his cause.

1313   Emperor Henry VII dies, having achieved little.

1315   Dante is offered amnesty permitting him to return to Florence, but he rejects it on account of the humiliating terms.

1319   *Purgatorio* is completed, or mostly so.

1321   Dante completes *Paradiso* and, thus, the whole of the *Divine Comedy*.

        In September, having caught malaria during the journey back to Ravenna from a diplomatic mission in Venice, he dies.

1829   A tomb for Dante is completed in Florence, in the Church of Santa Croce. However, it is never used because the custodians of Dante's tomb in Ravenna refuse to let his remains be taken to Florence.

2008   The city council of Florence, after seven centuries, finally rescinds the condemnation and banishment of one of the city's most famous citizens.

INTRODUCTION

WHEN DANTE SET OUT ON HIS JOURNEY INTO HELL THROUGH THE medium of poetry—the *Inferno*–then ascended the mount of Purgatory and went on to the heavens and his ultimate vision of the cosmos in Paradise, he laid out a radical new path into human feeling, understanding, and language, which has been followed ever since by readers and artists. For T. S. Eliot, there were two supreme masters of the Western imagination: Dante and Shakespeare. The *Inferno, Purgatorio*, and *Paradiso* make up the *Divine Comedy*, a comedy because it begins in uncertainty and concludes in complete spiritual fulfillment—the ultimate happy ending. In writing this epic poem in the early fourteenth century, Dante brought together, and made his own, all the contemporary main streams of thought regarding politics, society, philosophy, and above all, the Christian faith. Growing up in Florence in the late thirteenth century, he wrote love poetry, gradually moving the boundaries of that form with the creation of a poetic language aiming to capture the full meaning of divine love. He did not write the *Comedy* in Latin, the language of high aspiration hitherto, but in the vernacular, the Italian he had learned from the cradle on. This was another reason to call his work a comedy, as it was written in a "low," everyday language. But doing so gave him the scope to connect the workings of God with contemporary human experience; to emerge from the shadow of his great Latin forebear and guide, Virgil, and create afresh; and to establish the idea that a renewed Roman Empire could bring order and dignity to a strife-torn Italy, as his poetry conferred order and dignity on the lived language, Italian.

In Florence (his, by turn, beloved and hated home city), he came to see nothing but a travesty of political and social order and of human dignity. He, Dante Alighieri, was born there in 1265, into a minor aristocratic clan, his parents dying while he was young. He made his way from his teens onward in the intellectual circles that had begun to flourish in that wealthy, rapidly evolving city, making a name for himself writing love poetry in the Provençal and Sicilian styles that had become fashionable. He had a number of love objects for his sonnets and canzoni (lyrics to be sung), though one among them—Beatrice Portinari—made an overwhelming impression on him; he first caught sight of her when he was nine years old and she eight. Years later, she would emerge in the *Comedy* as fully spiritualized, inspiring sacred love and understanding combined, almost the incarnation of theology. But that transformation would come when the poet was in middle age. In the meantime, Dante married Gemma di Manetto Donati, who came from another Florentine aristocratic clan, and started a family. (The year during which the marriage took place is not known for certain, though it probably occurred in 1285.) Beatrice also married, but died at the age of twenty-four in 1290, leaving a determination in Dante to write of her "that which has never been written of any woman."[1] The year before, Dante had been a soldier, fighting at the Battle of Campaldino, a victory for his city as part of the Guelf (pro-papal) forces against the Ghibelline (pro-imperial) city of Arezzo, but he then turned back to religious study (there has been a suggestion that he thought of joining a religious order) and writing. By 1295, he had finished *La vita nuova*, commentaries on his own poems from the previous decade or so, built on an autobiographical framework; it was written in Italian rather than Latin, and its theme was love, showing how the erotic could be sublimated into philosophical and spiritual meaning—a portent of the greater work to come. That same year, he also entered politics. His career thrived, but at a bad time, for the Guelfs of Florence, having ejected the city's Ghibellines nearly two generations before, had themselves split into two factions, the Black Guelfs and the White Guelfs. As so often happens in faction fighting, the original loyalties—of Guelfs to the Pope, and Ghibellines to the Holy Roman emperor—had been lost amidst blood feuds and power struggles. Dante, by family origin a White Guelf, was elected as one of the six ruling priors of Florence in June 1300, but a struggle ensued in which the Black Guelfs triumphed; as a result, in 1302 Dante was banished from Florence, finally being sentenced to burning should he return. He never did. He was offered amnesty in 1315, but it was on humiliating terms, which he rejected. Instead, he wandered the cities of northern Italy, staying for periods wherever he found patronage and support from friendly rulers who welcomed the cultural luster he brought. In 1321, returning from an embassy to Venice on behalf of his latest host (the ruler of Ravenna), he caught malaria; he died during the night of September 13–14.

The dislocation of exile can spark creativity, and Dante, reacting to the destruction of his home life and the civic bonds that had seemed crucial to life itself, searched for an ever deeper understanding of the foundations of human existence and the means to express them. During the years 1302 to 1305, he wrote *De vulgari eloquentia,* a Latin treatise defending the use of the vernacular. From 1304 to 1307, he composed *Il convivio,* a "banquet" (the translation of *convivio*) of ideas, in which he served up philosophy, seeking to grasp the *intelligenze,* the intelligences that govern the heavens; this treatise was written in an Italian digestible to those in active life who were too preoccupied to read Latin. Dante was the theorist, as well as a practical creator, of modern Italian, binding a cultural community together in a way that proved so elusive politically. It is also likely that he wrote for performance—his works intended to be delivered in public lectures, which explains much of their form—rather than solely for circulation in manuscript. And he continued his reading in ever greater depth: Aristotle (in translation via Arabic), Cicero, and Virgil, among those from the classical world, and Saint Augustine, Boethius, Saint Thomas Aquinas—the great systematic thinkers of the Christian world. Gradually Dante absorbed these influences into his own unrivaled system of thought, encompassing the world and the heavens.

The *Inferno,* this first part, or canticle, of the *Comedy,* was known by 1315, and was most likely begun in 1306 or 1307. *Purgatorio* and *Paradiso* were written in the decade or so before Dante's death. At first it was feared that the final canticle, *Paradiso,* was unfinished but, as the story has it, Dante visited one of his sons in a dream and directed him to the cupboard where the final cantos had been stashed before he set off on his last journey to Venice.

Dante believed in the mystic significance of numbers, by which the universe was structured. For him, the number three and its multiples were of greatest significance, as in the Trinity, and Dante associated the number nine with Beatrice. Thus, he structured the *Comedy* in threes; each canticle is divided into thirty-three cantos, with the *Inferno* having one extra by way of an introduction. The extra canto in the *Inferno* enabled him to reach a total of one hundred, a perfect number.

Dante wrote his early poetry in what he called the *dolce stil novo*, or "sweet new style." It was developed by poets such as Guido Guinizelli and Guido Cavalcanti, Dante's immediate predecessors. From them he learned how to capture, in refined language and metaphor, the interior state of nuanced feeling inspired by a beautiful woman, gradually making this sweet new style, and its transfigured eroticism, expressive of philosophy and spiritual love. He varied his tone in the *Comedy*—not least in the pathos, horror, and anger of the *Inferno*—and that extended his stylistic mastery beyond all precedents in medieval literature. He also used dialogue between Virgil and "Dante"—his fictional alter ego in the poem—as well as between this same alter ego and the sinners encountered by him, in a way that was novel for the time, opening up great possibilities for drama, human interaction, and the exploration of ideas.

The sound of the language is a key aspect of the *Comedy*, especially of course, when read aloud. Italian, as molded by Dante from Tuscan and other dialects, has a great range and potential for rhyme through its musical word endings. An essential feature of the style in the *Comedy* is *terza rima*. In a *terzina*, a three-line unit, each line consists of eleven syllables, linked together through rhyme (the scheme being *aba, bcb, cdc,* and so on), drawing the reader ever onward from one thought, one image, to the next. A translator can convey much of the original, as Henry Wadsworth Longfellow has done here, though inevitably, and famously as all translators do, has to betray the original, not least when it comes to the extraordinarily structured and enlivened control of the original Italian that sets Dante apart.

Longfellow's translation was a labor of love. It took pretty much three decades, up to 1867, and became something of an obsession. He drew other writers into the project, such as Charles Eliot Norton and James Russell Lowell, and formed the Dante Club at Harvard, which later became the Dante Society of America. The impetus he gave is still felt in Dante studies across the United States, particularly in the Dante projects at Dartmouth, Columbia, and Yale.

Despite Longfellow's efforts, however, a reader may be dismayed by a feeling of remoteness from Dante, a sensation perhaps intensified when contemplating the intellectual universe in which Dante lived through his absorption in the great classical authors and the systematizers of Christian belief, writers who now rarely make up our general reading. However, Dante was always ready to help his readers with guidance as to how to read him, as in the commentaries on his own poetry in works such as *La vita nuova* and *Il convivio*. And as the *Inferno* (set in the year 1300, during the hours approaching Easter) opens, we find Dante at the midpoint of his life, age thirty-five, in a dark and mysterious wood, feeling terrified and confused himself. Dante the author has given us Dante the protagonist to be our proxy on a journey in which that terror and confusion will gradually be transmuted into an understanding of the divine plan and the realization of divine love, in contrast with human love gone wrong. As Dante enters Hell, he reads above the gate the famous words "All hope abandon, ye who enter in!" But that statement applies only to those who have no faith. It does not apply to Dante, and we readers, in a literary if not theological frame, place faith in him to represent us in finding a way through these darkest recesses of the imagination and our own lack of understanding, to come out on the other side enlightened. For his journey, Dante the protagonist has guides—Beatrice, who will meet him in *Purgatorio* and guide him into *Paradiso*, being one of them. But, for his travels through the *Inferno*, Beatrice has summoned the assistance of Virgil, the great poet of classical Rome.

Virgil leads Dante through the perilous terrain of Hell before ascending the mount of Purgatory where Beatrice takes over. He acts as a protector, an instructor, and a father figure. In one dimension, Virgil stands for Reason as Beatrice does for Faith, but these are complex characters, not just ciphers. Dante the protagonist asks our questions for us, and Virgil answers them. As a poet, too, Dante looked to Virgil as his role model, the author of the epic the *Aeneid*, in which the hero Aeneas flees a burning Troy, eventually to become the founder of Rome. As one stage of his journey, Aeneas descends into Hades (to seek counsel from his father, Anchises), as Dante descends into Hell. Virgil was the master poet who had brought Latin to a pitch of perfection, and Dante intended to achieve a similar goal with regard to Italian. With the *Aeneid*, Virgil had written the great secular epic, establishing in Dante's view the key values of Roman civilization. In his fourth Eclogue, Virgil had appeared to prophesy the coming of Christ when he talked of a return to a golden age of justice and peace. But Virgil himself never had faith in Christ, so in Dante's work, he dwells in Limbo, a neutral area for those not baptized, the first circle before a descent into the Inferno proper, with its nine circles in all, narrowing down to the center of the earth and filled with populations of unrepentant sinners, their sins more grievous circle by circle.

The connection with Rome, which Virgil represented, was vital for Dante. He saw the triumphant establishment of the Roman Empire and the coming of Christ as two connected events, one bringing the secular order to perfection and the other bringing spiritual redemption. Above all, the empire was the guarantor of peace, in which the human intellect and, through that, spiritual understanding could flourish. In Dante's day, German kings laid claim to be Holy Roman emperors, and Dante longed for their triumph over factious, continually warring Italy. He wrote a theoretical treatise, *Monarchia*, justifying such imperial rule. In that work—as in his letters, much of his political activity, and the terrible fate that he imagined for a number of popes in the *Inferno*—he sought to combat the secular power of the papacy, which he saw as a betrayal of true spiritual leadership and the most fundamental obstacle to peace. His ire was directed in particular against the pope at the time of his exile, Boniface VIII, whose meddling in Florence had helped divide the city rather than unite it as a good shepherd should, and who had disastrously claimed sovereignty over emperors, kings, and the whole world. Dante destined Pope Boniface, along with other popes and clerics who made illicit profit out of their sacred offices, to one of the lowest circles of Hell, the eighth out of nine, to be buried headfirst in holes in the rock, legs emerging ignominiously, flames burning on the soles of their feet.

On his journey through Hell, Dante meets a panoply of sinners from Christian and classical history and legend, as well as some of his Italian contemporaries, chief among them being Florentines and neighboring Tuscans. One individual falling into that latter group is Vanni Fucci, a murderer and thief from Pistoia. Dante portrays Vanni maliciously, foretelling divisions worsening in Florence and closing with an obscene gesture directed at God—whereupon two serpents bind Vanni and he burns to ashes, only to be reconstituted so that his torments may continue. At first reading of descriptions such as this, it looks as though Dante was settling a great number of personal scores, and perhaps he was, but there was always method in his wrath. These sinners were those whose factiousness and greed had severed the civic bonds and wrecked Florence and Tuscany, and Dante's own life there, undermining that most precious thing—peace.

The images of suffering in the *Inferno* are among the most vivid in Western art and draw upon all forms of artistic and personal experience. Dante varies the tone of his descriptions in a carefully controlled way that gives relief, as well as intensity, to the emotional response of the reader. In Malebolge ("evil ditches") deep down in Hell, where the fraudulent and malicious are to be found, Dante and Virgil come across a group of threatening demons from whom they must flee. But these demons are also comic figures, bickering, falling over, and outwitted. Dante may have found such slapstick in the popular religious street theater accompanying festivals, just as he absorbed various images of Hell from frescoes and mosaics. He drew upon, and created, mythology—an example being the winged creature Geryon, bearing the face of an honest man (really a fraudulent show of honesty), the body of a mythical reptile, and the paws of a lion, assembled together with a sting in its tail; Virgil commands the monster to bear Dante and him on its back in circular flight down past an otherwise impassable waterfall to the circle of fraud.

In contrast with these broader strokes, there is great poignancy in many of Dante's images. Suicides, for instance, appear as trees, on the boughs of which they will hang their own bodies, which they rejected, following the Last Judgment. Dante discovers them when he breaks off a twig, which causes bleeding and elicits an outcry of pain. He sees some of himself perhaps in Ulysses, who also went in quest of ultimate knowledge and who sailed past the Pillars of Hercules until he found the mount of Purgatory, whereupon his ship was sucked into a whirlpool with the loss of all on board. But Dante is contrasting the prudence that he aspired to with the overweening cleverness of Ulysses, and he is making explicit the danger of intellect unconstrained by virtue. Many of the sinners engage Dante's and the reader's sympathy, such as Paolo and Francesca, doomed lovers condemned forever to be wafted on the winds of their passion, a subject that would later become a favorite for Romantic artists. Such artists were also fascinated by Ugolino, who had acted treacherously but was, himself, in turn betrayed, meeting the dread fate on earth of being sealed in a room with his two sons and two grandsons—and watching them die from starvation until he himself perished. One of the sons offered his flesh to his starving father; Dante's verse leaves it ambiguous as to what Ugolino did. In Hell, Ugolino continually gnaws the head of Archbishop Ruggieri, who had ordered the room sealed. In less gruesome but also ambiguous mode, among the sodomites Dante finds his old teacher Brunetto Latini, whose inspiration and "dear and good paternal image" he clearly continues to revere and whom he cannot quite believe is to be found there. Such sympathy in Dante the protagonist has resonated with later readers in a Romantic or liberal age, and is a means for us to find our way into the poem— though it can be misleading. Dante the author is showing the fallibility of Dante the protagonist in experiencing such sympathy. The underlying sense of the whole narrative is that all such sinners in the *Inferno* are there by divine judgment, the ultimate good, however mysterious that judgment might be.

In Joan Ferrante's words, "Dante shows . . . that we choose in our acts to inhabit the city of Hell, to turn our city into Hell."[2] This is symbolized in the imagery of punishment Dante employs. The poet Bertran de Born is depicted as carrying his own severed head; during his life, he caused conflict within the family of King Henry II of England, so just as he parted members of a family from one another, in this *contrapasso*, as it is termed—where the sin rebounds on the sinner—his head is parted from his body. Dante's moral scheme was based on Christian teaching and its absorption of the ethics of Aristotle, for whom the golden mean was the measure—not too much, not too little. Thus, for instance, spendthrifts and misers are both to be found in the *Inferno* for misuse of money—in excess and in deficiency, respectively. A particular feature in Dante's ranking of vice that some find surprising is that fraud is deemed worse than violence. Dante followed the great Latin writer and moralist Cicero in this. Bodily injury was bad, but for Cicero, the destruction of trust, the sacred bonds between human beings, was worse, and totally self-defeating.

With this scheme in mind, Dante's journey through the *Inferno* serves as a dramatized guide to sin, or in secular terms, human failing and frailty, the harm of self and others. Structuring the drama is a powerful sense of place; the topography of the *Inferno* is key to understanding it, with the dark and savage wood near the entrance, its rivers derived from classical mythology, and its nine circles going deeper, one after another, in sin. In the medieval period, with books expensive and scarce, the art of memory was cultivated, one technique being to imagine places in which a series of objects were placed, each one standing for an idea or fact; to recall anything, one visited the relevant places in the imagination. These could be "memory palaces," but in this case, the sites embodying the memory of sin are the circles of Hell.

In the dark wood where Dante first finds himself, he encounters three creatures: a leopard, a lion, and a she-wolf. The meaning of each is still much debated, but the leopard may be lust, unbridled desire, and the lion ambition and pride. The emaciated wolf is the most dangerous, representing ravenous greed, and Dante cannot escape this creature, except by accepting Virgil's guidance down into Hell. The first circle is Limbo, where dwell those who were virtuous during their lives, but were not redeemed through baptism and faith, such as Virgil. In the next four circles, descending deeper from one to the next, are those who lacked control over their natural instincts, who abandoned reason, the highest human faculty. There are the lustful, such as Paolo and Francesca in the second circle; the gluttonous in the third circle;

spendthrifts and misers in the fourth circle; the wrathful in the fifth. Then, farther down, Virgil and Dante enter the city of Dis, where those who have engendered strife are to be found. There, in the sixth circle, are the heretics, who have not just distorted God-given reason but also caused terrible conflict. In the seventh circle are those who have been violent—against others and their property; against the self, as in suicide; and against God, either directly, as in blasphemy, or against the nature and procreation He ordained, as in two different forms of sterility, as Dante saw it: sodomy and usury. Much deeper, beneath a precipitous barrier and waterfall, lies the eighth circle, Malebolge, with its ten divisions, or "ditches," where fraud is the sin. The culmination is the ninth circle, where treachery—the destruction of trust and the most basic of human bonds—is depicted. Deepest of all, and most treacherous of all, is Lucifer, surrounded by Cocytus, a frozen lake of tears. He sits immobile, except for the eternal flapping of his hideous wings and the freezing winds they create, his three heads gnawing on the three archetypal traitors, Brutus and Cassius, and Judas Iscariot, those who had betrayed Caesar and Christ, subverting the Roman Empire and Christianity, the two essential conditions for human well-being. Crawling over Lucifer, who is devoid of feeling, Dante and Virgil emerge at the foot of the mount of Purgatory at dawn on Easter Sunday, their journey through Hell complete.

The meaning to be derived from this journey has been debated for centuries, and no doubt will continue to be for centuries more. It is not simply poetic allegory, with Virgil standing for Reason and Beatrice for Faith, but rather it is multilayered in its significance, like biblical allegory, which can be read in a fourfold way—as straightforward narrative; with a meaning relating one set of events or people to another; with a moral meaning; and with an anagogical (mystical) meaning. But the power of Dante's storytelling may make "decoding" it sometimes a distraction from an experience that Erich Auerbach argued was the first sign of what was to become the modern novel. In the *Comedy*, only there in the Middle Ages do we meet "man not as a remote legendary hero, not as an abstract or anecdotal representative of an ethical type, but man as we know him in his living historical reality, the concrete individual in his unity and wholeness."[3]

Dante's journey was mapped and pored over in great detail by commentators immediately following the poet's death. The most significant of these individuals was Giovanni Boccaccio, who first termed the *Comedy* the *Divine Comedy*. There was a lull in interest during the later Renaissance, but a marked revival occurred from the eighteenth century on, and alongside scholarship and literature, there was a flood of paintings and sculpture—Auguste Rodin's *Gates of Hell* being among the most outstanding—as well as, in more recent times, many movies, installations, and even video games. (It must remain uncertain in which circle Dante would have placed obsessive video gamers.) Each age will make of the *Inferno* and the rest of the *Comedy* what it will. But the real reward lies in journeying attentively with Dante, letting him and his so subtly crafted narrative elucidate for us the rich thought world of the Middle Ages as brought together and reimagined by its greatest poet. And, given Dante's enduring insight into human frailties and human relationships, we find ourselves emerging with him into our own world.

ᜒ CANTO I ᜒ

*The Dark Forest—The Hill of Difficulty—The Panther,
the Lion, and the Wolf—Virgil*

MIDWAY UPON THE JOURNEY OF OUR LIFE[1]
I found myself within a forest dark,
For the straightforward pathway had been lost.

Ah me! how hard a thing it is to say
    What was this forest savage, rough, and stern,   5
    Which in the very thought renews the fear.

So bitter is it, death is little more;
    But of the good to treat, which there I found,
    Speak will I of the other things I saw there.

I cannot well repeat how there I entered,   10
    So full was I of slumber at the moment
    In which I had abandoned the true way.

But after I had reached a mountain's foot,
    At that point where the valley terminated,
    Which had with consternation pierced my heart,   15

Upward I looked, and I beheld its shoulders,
    Vested already with that planet's rays
    Which leadeth others right by every road.

Then was the fear a little quieted
    That in my heart's lake had endured throughout   20
    The night, which I had passed so piteously.

And even as he, who, with distressful breath,
    Forth issued from the sea upon the shore,
    Turns to the water perilous and gazes;

So did my soul, that still was fleeing onward,   25
    Turn itself back to re-behold the pass
    Which never yet a living person left.

After my weary body I had rested,
    The way resumed I on the desert slope,
    So that the firm foot ever was the lower.   30

And lo! almost where the ascent began,
    A panther[2] light and swift exceedingly,
    Which with a spotted skin was covered o'er!

And never moved she from before my face,
    Nay, rather did impede so much my way,   35
    That many times I to return had turned.

The time was the beginning of the morning,
    And up the sun was mounting with those stars
    That with him were, what time the Love Divine

At first in motion set those beauteous things;   40
    So were to me occasion of good hope,
    The variegated skin of that wild beast,

The hour of time, and the delicious season;
    But not so much, that did not give me fear
    A lion's aspect[3] which appeared to me.   45

He seemed as if against me he were coming
    With head uplifted, and with ravenous hunger,
    So that it seemed the air was afraid of him;

And a she-wolf,[4] that with all hungerings
    Seemed to be laden in her meagerness,   50
    And many folk has caused to live forlorn!

She brought upon me so much heaviness,
    With the affright that from her aspect came,
    That I the hope relinquished of the height.

And as he is who willingly acquires,   55
    And the time comes that causes him to lose,
    Who weeps in all his thoughts and is despondent,

E'en such made me that beast withouten peace,
    Which, coming on against me by degrees
    Thrust me back thither where the sun is silent.   60

While I was rushing downward to the lowland,
    Before mine eyes did one present himself,[5]
    Who seemed from long-continued silence hoarse.

When I beheld him in the desert vast,
    "Have pity on me," unto him I cried,   65
    "Whiche'er thou art, or shade or real man!"

He answered me: "Not man; man once I was,
    And both my parents were of Lombardy,
    And Mantuans by country both of them.

Sub Julio was I born, though it was late,   70
    And lived at Rome under the good Augustus,
    During the time of false and lying gods.[6]

A poet was I, and I sang that just
    Son of Anchises, who came forth from Troy,
    After that Ilion[7] the superb was burned.   75

But thou, why goest thou back to such annoyance?
    Why climb'st thou not the Mount Delectable,
    Which is the source and cause of every joy?"

"Now, art thou that Virgilius and that fountain
    Which spreads abroad so wide a river of speech?"   80
    I made response to him with bashful forehead.

"O, of the other poets honor and light,
    Avail me the long study and great love
    That have impelled me to explore thy volume!

Thou art my master, and my author thou,   85
    Thou art alone the one from whom I took
    The beautiful style that has done honor to me.

Behold the beast, for which I have turned back;
    Do thou protect me from her, famous Sage,
    For she doth make my veins and pulses tremble."   90

"Thee it behoves to take another road,"
    Responded he, when he beheld me weeping,
    "If from this savage place thou wouldst escape;

Because this beast, at which thou criest out,
    Suffers not any one to pass her way,   95
    But so doth harass him, that she destroys him;

And has a nature so malign and ruthless,
    That never doth she glut her greedy will,
    And after food is hungrier than before.

Many the animals with whom she weds,   100
    And more they shall be still, until the Greyhound[8]
    Comes, who shall make her perish in her pain.

He shall not feed on either earth or pelf,
    But upon wisdom, and on love and virtue;
    'Twixt Feltro and Feltro[9] shall his nation be;   105

Of that low Italy shall he be the savior,
    On whose account the maid Camilla died,
    Euryalus, Turnus, Nisus,[10] of their wounds;

Through every city shall he hunt her down,
    Until he shall have driven her back to Hell,   110
    There from whence envy first did let her loose.

Therefore I think and judge it for thy best
    Thou follow me, and I will be thy guide,
    And lead thee hence through the eternal place,

Where thou shalt hear the desperate lamentations,   115
    Shalt see the ancient spirits disconsolate,
    Who cry out each one for the second death;

And thou shalt see those who contented are
    Within the fire, because they hope to come,
    Whene'er it may be, to the blessed people;   120

To whom, then, if thou wishest to ascend,
    A soul shall be for that than I more worthy;
    With her at my departure I will leave thee;[11]

Because that Emperor, who reigns above,
    In that I was rebellious to his law,   125
    Wills that through me none come into his city.

He governs everywhere, and there he reigns;
    There is his city and his lofty throne;
    O happy he whom thereto he elects!"

And I to him: "Poet, I thee entreat,   130
    By that same God whom thou didst never know,
    So that I may escape this woe and worse,

Thou wouldst conduct me there where thou hast said,
    That I may see the portal of Saint Peter,
    And those thou makest so disconsolate."   135

Then he moved on, and I behind him followed.

⊰ CANTO II ⊱

The Descent—Dante's Protest and Virgil's Appeal—
The Intercession of the Three Ladies Benedight

DAY WAS DEPARTING AND THE EMBROWNED AIR
Released the animals that are on earth
From their fatigues; and I the only one

Made myself ready to sustain the war,
    Both of the way and likewise of the woe,   5
    Which memory that errs not shall retrace.

O Muses, O high genius, now assist me!
    O memory, that didst write down what I saw,
    Here thy nobility shall be manifest!

And I began: "Poet, who guidest me,   10
    Regard my manhood, if it be sufficient,
    Ere to the arduous pass thou dost confide me.

Thou sayest, that of Silvius the parent,[1]
    While yet corruptible, unto the world
    Immortal went, and was there bodily.   15

But if the adversary of all evil
    Was courteous, thinking of the high effect
    That issue would from him, and who, and what,

7

To men of intellect unmeet it seems not;
    For he was of great Rome, and of her empire   20
    In the empyreal heaven as father chosen;

The which and what, wishing to speak the truth,
    Were stablished as the holy place, wherein
    Sits the successor of the greatest Peter.

Upon this journey, whence thou givest him vaunt,   25
    Things did he hear, which the occasion were
    Both of his victory and the papal mantle.

Thither went afterwards the Chosen Vessel,
    To bring back comfort thence unto that Faith,
    Which of salvation's way is the beginning.   30

But I, why thither come, or who concedes it?
    I not Æneas am, I am not Paul,[2]
    Nor I, nor others, think me worthy of it.

Therefore, if I resign myself to come,
    I fear the coming may be ill-advised;   35
    Thou'rt wise, and knowest better than I speak."

And as he is, who unwills what he willed,
    And by new thoughts doth his intention change,
    So that from his design he quite withdraws,

Such I became, upon that dark hillside,   40
    Because, in thinking, I consumed the emprise,
    Which was so very prompt in the beginning.

"If I have well thy language understood,"
    Replied that shade of the Magnanimous,
    "Thy soul attainted is with cowardice,   45

Which many times a man encumbers so,
　　It turns him back from honored enterprise,
　　As false sight doth a beast, when he is shy.

That thou mayst free thee from this apprehension,
　　I'll tell thee why I came, and what I heard　　　　50
　　At the first moment when I grieved for thee.

Among those was I who are in suspense,
　　And a fair, saintly Lady called to me
　　In such wise, I besought her to command me.

Her eyes where shining brighter than the Star;　　　55
　　And she began to say, gentle and low,
　　With voice angelical, in her own language:

'O spirit courteous of Mantua,
　　Of whom the fame still in the world endures,
　　And shall endure, long-lasting as the world;　　　60

A friend of mine, and not the friend of fortune,
　　Upon the desert slope is so impeded
　　Upon his way, that he has turned through terror,

And may, I fear, already be so lost,
　　That I too late have risen to his succor,　　　　65
　　From that which I have heard of him in Heaven.

Bestir thee now, and with thy speech ornate,
　　And with what needful is for his release,
　　Assist him so, that I may be consoled.

Beatrice am I, who do bid thee go;　　　　　　70
　　I come from there, where I would fain return;
　　Love moved me, which compelleth me to speak.

When I shall be in presence of my Lord,
　　Full often will I praise thee unto him.'
　　Then paused she, and thereafter I began:　　　　　75

'O Lady of virtue, thou alone through whom
　　The human race exceedeth all contained
　　Within the heaven that has the lesser circles,[3]

So grateful unto me is thy commandment,
　　To obey, if 'twere already done, were late;　　　　80
　　No farther need'st thou ope to me thy wish.

But the cause tell me why thou dost not shun
　　The here descending down into this center,
　　From the vast place thou burnest to return to.'

'Since thou wouldst fain so inwardly discern,　　　　85
　　Briefly will I relate,' she answered me,
　　'Why I am not afraid to enter here.

Of those things only should one be afraid
　　Which have the power of doing others harm;
　　Of the rest, no; because they are not fearful.　　　90

God in his mercy such created me
　　That misery of yours attains me not,
　　Nor any flame assails me of this burning.

A gentle Lady[4] is in Heaven, who grieves
　　At this impediment, to which I send thee,　　　　95
　　So that stern judgment there above is broken.

In her entreaty she besought Lucìa,[5]
　　And said, "Thy faithful one now stands in need
　　Of thee, and unto thee I recommend him."

Lucìa, foe of all that cruel is,   100
    Hastened away, and came unto the place
    Where I was sitting with the ancient Rachel.[6]

"Beatrice" said she, "the true praise of God,
    Why succorest thou not him, who loved thee so,
    For thee he issued from the vulgar herd?   105

Dost thou not hear the pity of his plaint?
    Dost thou not see the death that combats him
    Beside that flood, where ocean has no vaunt?"

Never were persons in the world so swift
    To work their weal and to escape their woe,   110
    As I, after such words as these were uttered,

Came hither downward from my blessed seat,
    Confiding in thy dignified discourse,
    Which honors thee, and those who've listened to it.'

After she thus had spoken unto me,   115
    Weeping, her shining eyes she turned away;
    Whereby she made me swifter in my coming;

And unto thee I came, as she desired;
    I have delivered thee from that wild beast,
    Which barred the beautiful mountain's short ascent.   120

What is it, then? Why, why dost thou delay?
    Why is such baseness bedded in thy heart?
    Daring and hardihood why hast thou not,

Seeing that three such Ladies benedight[7]
    Are caring for thee in the court of Heaven,   125
    And so much good my speech doth promise thee?"

Even as the flowerets, by nocturnal chill,
  Bowed down and closed, when the sun whitens them,
  Uplift themselves all open on their stems;

Such I became with my exhausted strength,   130
  And such good courage to my heart there coursed,
  That I began, like an intrepid person:

"O she compassionate, who succored me,
  And courteous thou, who hast obeyed so soon
  The words of truth which she addressed to thee!   135

Thou hast my heart so with desire disposed
  To the adventure, with these words of thine,
  That to my first intent I have returned.

Now go, for one sole will is in us both,
  Thou Leader, and thou Lord, and Master thou."   140
  Thus said I to him; and when he had moved,

I entered on the deep and savage way.

⊰ CANTO III ⊱

The Gate of Hell—The Inefficient or Indifferent—Pope Celestine V—
The Shores of Acheron—Charon—The Earthquake and the Swoon

"THROUGH ME THE WAY IS TO THE CITY DOLENT;[1]
Through me the way is to eternal dole;
Through me the way among the people lost.

Justice incited my sublime Creator;
   Created me divine Omnipotence,   5
   The highest Wisdom and the primal Love.

Before me there were no created things,
   Only eterne, and I eternal last.
   All hope abandon, ye who enter in!"

These words in somber color I beheld   10
   Written upon the summit of a gate;
   Whence I: "Their sense is, Master, hard to me!"

And he to me, as one experienced:
   "Here all suspicion needs must be abandoned,
   All cowardice must needs be here extinct.   15

We to the place have come, where I have told thee
   Thou shalt behold the people dolorous
   Who have foregone the good of intellect."

13

And after he had laid his hand on mine
    With joyful mien, whence I was comforted,   20
    He led me in among the secret things.

There sighs, complaints, and ululations loud
    Resounded through the air without a star,
    Whence I, at the beginning, wept thereat.

Languages diverse, horrible dialects,   25
    Accents of anger, words of agony,
    And voices high and hoarse, with sound of hands,

Made up a tumult that goes whirling on
    For ever in that air for ever black,
    Even as the sand doth, when the whirlwind breathes.   30

And I, who had my head with horror bound,
    Said: "Master, what is this which now I hear?
    What folk is this, which seems by pain so vanquished?"

And he to me: "This miserable mode
    Maintain the melancholy souls of those   35
    Who lived withouten infamy or praise.

Commingled are they with that caitiff[2] choir
    Of Angels, who have not rebellious been,
    Nor faithful were to God, but were for self.

The heavens expelled them, not to be less fair;   40
    Nor them the nethermore abyss receives,
    For glory none the damned would have from them."

And I: "O Master, what so grievous is
    To these, that maketh them lament so sore?"
    He answered: "I will tell thee very briefly.   45

These have no longer any hope of death;
    And this blind life of theirs is so debased,
    They envious are of every other fate.

No fame of them the world permits to be;
    Misericord and Justice both disdain them.   50
    Let us not speak of them, but look, and pass."

And I, who looked again, beheld a banner,
    Which, whirling round, ran on so rapidly,
    That of all pause it seemed to me indignant;

And after it there came so long a train   55
    Of people, that I ne'er would have believed
    That ever Death so many had undone.

When some among them I had recognized,
    I looked, and I beheld the shade of him
    Who made through cowardice the great refusal.   60

Forthwith I comprehended, and was certain,
    That this the sect was of the caitiff wretches
    Hateful to God and to his enemies.

These miscreants, who never were alive,
    Were naked, and were stung exceedingly   65
    By gadflies and by hornets that were there.

These did their faces irrigate with blood,
    Which, with their tears commingled, at their feet
    By the disgusting worms was gathered up.

And when to gazing farther I betook me.   70
    People I saw on a great river's bank;
    Whence said I: "Master, now vouchsafe to me,

That I may know who these are, and what law
   Makes them appear so ready to pass over,
   As I discern athwart the dusky light."   75

And he to me: "These things shall all be known
   To thee, as soon as we our footsteps stay
   Upon the dismal shore of Acheron."[3]

Then with mine eyes ashamed and downward cast,
   Fearing my words might irksome be to him,   80
   From speech refrained I till we reached the river.

And lo! towards us coming in a boat
   An old man, hoary with the hair of eld,
   Crying: "Woe unto you, ye souls depraved!

Hope nevermore to look upon the heavens;   85
   I come to lead you to the other shore,
   To the eternal shades in heat and frost.

And thou, that yonder standest, living soul,
   Withdraw thee from these people, who are dead!"
   But when he saw that I did not withdraw,   90

He said: "By other ways, by other ports
   Thou to the shore shalt come, not here, for passage;
   A lighter vessel needs must carry thee."

And unto him the Guide: "Vex thee not, Charon;[4]
   It is so willed there where is power to do   95
   That which is willed; and farther question not."

Thereat were quieted the fleecy cheeks
   Of him the ferryman of the livid fen,
   Who round about his eyes had wheels of flame.

But all those souls who weary were and naked   100
    Their color changed and gnashed their teeth together,
    As soon as they had heard those cruel words.

God they blasphemed and their progenitors,
    The human race, the place, the time, the seed
    Of their engendering and of their birth!   105

Thereafter all together they drew back,
    Bitterly weeping, to the accursed shore,
    Which waiteth every man who fears not God.

Charon the demon, with the eyes of glede,[5]
    Beckoning to them, collects them all together,   110
    Beats with his oar whoever lags behind.

As in the autumn-time the leaves fall off,
    First one and then another, till the branch
    Unto the earth surrenders all its spoils;

In similar wise the evil seed of Adam   115
    Throw themselves from that margin one by one,
    At signals, as a bird unto its lure.

So they depart across the dusky wave,
    And ere upon the other side they land,
    Again on this side a new troop assembles.   120

"My son," the courteous Master said to me,
    "All those who perish in the wrath of God
    Here meet together out of every land;

And ready are they to pass o'er the river,
    Because celestial Justice spurs them on,   125
    So that their fear is turned into desire.

This way there never passes a good soul;
　　And hence if Charon doth complain of thee,
　　Well mayst thou know now what his speech imports."

This being finished, all the dusk champaign[6]　　　　130
　　Trembled so violently, that of that terror
　　The recollection bathes me still with sweat.

The land of tears gave forth a blast of wind,
　　And fulminated a vermilion light,
　　Which overmastered in me every sense,　　　　135

And as a man whom sleep hath seized I fell.

⫷ CANTO IV ⫸

The First Circle, Limbo: Virtuous Pagans and the Unbaptized—
The Four Poets, Homer, Horace, Ovid, and Lucan—
The Noble Castle of Philosophy

BROKE THE DEEP LETHARGY WITHIN MY HEAD
A heavy thunder, so that I upstarted,
Like to a person who by force is wakened;

And round about I moved my rested eyes,
    Uprisen erect, and steadfastly I gazed,   5
    To recognize the place wherein I was.

True is it, that upon the verge I found me
    Of the abysmal valley dolorous,
    That gathers thunder of infinite ululations.

Obscure, profound it was, and nebulous,   10
    So that by fixing on its depths my sight
    Nothing whatever I discerned therein.

"Let us descend now into the blind world,"
    Began the Poet, pallid utterly;
    "I will be first, and thou shalt second be."   15

And I, who of his color was aware,
    Said: "How shall I come, if thou art afraid,
    Who'rt wont to be a comfort to my fears?"

And he to me: "The anguish of the people
    Who are below here in my face depicts   20
    That pity which for terror thou hast taken.

Let us go on, for the long way impels us."
    Thus he went in, and thus he made me enter
    The foremost circle that surrounds the abyss.[1]

There, as it seemed to me from listening,   25
    Were lamentations none, but only sighs,
    That tremble made the everlasting air.

And this arose from sorrow without torment,
    Which the crowds had, that many were and great,
    Of infants and of women and of men.   30

To me the Master good: "Thou dost not ask
    What spirits these, which thou beholdest, are?
    Now will I have thee know, ere thou go farther,

That they sinned not; and if they merit had,
    'Tis not enough, because they had not baptism   35
    Which is the portal of the Faith thou holdest;

And if they were before Christianity,
    In the right manner they adored not God;
    And among such as these am I myself.

For such defects, and not for other guilt,   40
    Lost are we, and are only so far punished,
    That without hope we live on in desire."

Great grief seized on my heart when this I heard,
    Because some people of much worthiness
    I knew, who in that Limbo were suspended.   45

"Tell me, my Master, tell me, thou my Lord,"
    Began I, with desire of being certain
    Of that Faith which o'ercometh every error,

"Came any one by his own merit hence,
    Or by another's, who was blessed thereafter?"   50
    And he, who understood my covert speech,

Replied: "I was a novice in this state,
    When I saw hither come a Mighty One,
    With sign of victory incoronate.

Hence he drew forth the shade of the First[2] Parent,   55
    And that of his son Abel, and of Noah,
    Of Moses the lawgiver, and the obedient

Abraham, patriarch, and David, king,
    Israel with his father and his children,
    And Rachel, for whose sake he did so much,   60

And others many, and he made them blessed;
    And thou must know, that earlier than these
    Never were any human spirits saved."

We ceased not to advance because he spake,
    But still were passing onward through the forest,   65
    The forest, say I, of thick-crowded ghosts.

Not very far as yet our way had gone
    This side the summit, when I saw a fire
    That overcame a hemisphere of darkness.

We were a little distant from it still,   70
    But not so far that I in part discerned not
    That honorable people held that place.

"O thou who honorest every art and science,
    Who may these be, which such great honor have,
    That from the fashion of the rest it parts them?"   75

And he to me: "The honorable name,
    That sounds of them above there in thy life,
    Wins grace in Heaven, that so advances them."

In the meantime a voice was heard by me:
    "All honor be to the preeminent Poet;   80
    His shade returns again, that was departed."

After the voice had ceased and quiet was,
    Four mighty shades I saw approaching us;
    Semblance had they nor sorrowful nor glad.

To say to me began my gracious Master: 85
    "Him with that falchion in his hand behold,
    Who comes before the three, even as their lord.

That one is Homer, Poet sovereign;
    He who comes next is Horace, the satirist;
    The third is Ovid, and the last is Lucan.[3]   90

Because to each of these with me applies
    The name that solitary voice proclaimed,
    They do me honor, and in that do well."

Thus I beheld assemble the fair school
    Of that lord of the song preeminent,   95
    Who o'er the others like an eagle soars.

When they together had discoursed somewhat,
    They turned to me with signs of salutation,
    And on beholding this, my Master smiled;

And more of honor still, much more, they did me,   100
    In that they made me one of their own band;
    So that the sixth was I, 'mid so much wit.

Thus we went on as far as to the light,
    Things saying 'tis becoming to keep silent,
    As was the saying of them where I was.   105

We came unto a noble castle's foot,
    Seven times encompassëd with lofty walls,
    Defended round by a fair rivulet;

This we passed over even as firm ground;
    Through portals seven I entered with these Sages;   110
    We came into a meadow of fresh verdure.

People were there with solemn eyes and slow,
    Of great authority in their countenance;
    They spake but seldom, and with gentle voices.

Thus we withdrew ourselves upon one side   115
    Into an opening luminous and lofty,
    So that they all of them were visible.

There opposite, upon the green enamel,
    Were pointed out to me the mighty spirits,
    Whom to have seen I feel myself exalted.   120

I saw Electra with companions many,
    'Mongst whom I knew both Hector and Æneas,
    Cæsar in armor with gerfalcon eyes;

I saw Camilla and Penthesilea
    On the other side, and saw the King Latinus,   125
    Who with Lavinia his daughter sat;

I saw that Brutus who drove Tarquin forth,
    Lucretia, Julia, Marcia, and Cornelia,
    And saw alone, apart, the Saladin.[4]

When I had lifted up my brows a little,   130
    The Master I beheld of those who know,
    Sit with his philosophic family.

All gaze upon him, and all do him honor.
    There I beheld both Socrates and Plato,
    Who nearer him before the others stand;   135

Democritus, who puts the world on chance,
    Diogenes, Anaxagoras, and Thales,
    Zeno, Empedocles, and Heraclitus;[5]

Of qualities I saw the good collector,
    Hight Dioscorides; and Orpheus saw I,   140
    Tully and Livy, and moral Seneca,

Euclid, geometrician, and Ptolemy,
    Galen, Hippocrates, and Avicenna,
    Averroes, who the great Comment[6] made.

I cannot all of them portray in full,   145
    Because so drives me onward the long theme,
    That many times the word comes short of fact.

The sixfold company in two divides;
    Another way my sapient Guide conducts me
    Forth from the quiet to the air that trembles;   150

And to a place I come where nothing shines.

⇥ CANTO V ⇤

The Second Circle: The Wanton—Minos—
The Infernal Hurricane—Francesca da Rimini

THUS I DESCENDED OUT OF THE FIRST CIRCLE
Down to the second, that less space begirds,
And so much greater dole, that goads to wailing.

There standeth Minos[1] horribly, and snarls;
   Examines the transgressions at the entrance;   5
   Judges, and sends according as he girds him.

I say, that when the spirit evil-born
   Cometh before him, wholly it confesses;
   And this discriminator of transgressions

Seeth what place in Hell is meet for it;   10
   Girds himself with his tail as many times
   As grades he wishes it should be thrust down.

Always before him many of them stand;
   They go by turns each one unto the judgment;
   They speak, and hear, and then are downward hurled. 15

"O thou, that to this dolorous hostelry
   Comest," said Minos to me, when he saw me,
   Leaving the practice of so great an office,

"Look how thou enterest, and in whom thou trustest;
    Let not the portal's amplitude deceive thee."   20
    And unto him my Guide: "Why criest thou too?

Do not impede his journey fate-ordained;
    It is so willed there where is power to do
    That which is willed; and ask no further question."

And now begin the dolesome notes to grow   25
    Audible unto me; now am I come
    There where much lamentation strikes upon me.

I came into a place mute of all light,
    Which bellows as the sea does in a tempest,
    If by opposing winds 't is combated.   30

The infernal hurricane that never rests
    Hurtles the spirits onward in its rapine;
    Whirling them round, and smiting, it molests them.

When they arrive before the precipice,
    There are the shrieks, the plaints, and the laments,   35
    There they blaspheme the puissance divine.

I understood that unto such a torment
    The carnal malefactors were condemned,
    Who reason subjugate to appetite.

And as the wings of starlings bear them on   40
    In the cold season in large band and full,
    So doth that blast the spirits maledict;

It hither, thither, downward, upward, drives them;
    No hope doth comfort them for evermore,
    Not of repose, but even of lesser pain.   45

And as the cranes go chanting forth their lays,
    Making in air a long line of themselves,
    So saw I coming, uttering lamentations,

Shadows borne onward by the aforesaid stress.
    Whereupon said I: "Master, who are those   50
    People, whom the black air so castigates?"

"The first of those, of whom intelligence
    Thou fain wouldst have," then said he unto me,
    "The empress was of many languages.

To sensual vices she was so abandoned,   55
    That lustful she made licit in her law,
    To remove the blame to which she had been led.

She is Semiramis, of whom we read
    That she succeeded Ninus, and was his spouse;
    She held the land which now the Sultan rules.   60

The next is she who killed herself for love,
    And broke faith with the ashes of Sichæus;
    Then Cleopatra the voluptuous."

Helen I saw, for whom so many ruthless
    Seasons revolved; and saw the great Achilles,   65
    Who at the last hour combated with Love.

Paris I saw, Tristan;[2] and more than a thousand
    Shades did he name and point out with his finger,
    Whom Love had separated from our life.

After that I had listened to my Teacher,   70
    Naming the dames of eld and cavaliers,
    Pity prevailed, and I was nigh bewildered.

And I began: "O Poet, willingly
    Speak would I to those two, who go together,
    And seem upon the wind to be so light."   75

And he to me: "Thou'lt mark, when they shall be
    Nearer to us; and then do thou implore them
    By love which leadeth them, and they will come."

Soon as the wind in our direction sways them,
    My voice uplift I: "O ye weary souls!   80
    Come speak to us, if no one interdicts it."

As turtledoves, called onward by desire,
    With open and steady wings to the sweet nest
    Fly through the air by their volition borne,

So came they from the band where Dido is,   85
    Approaching us athwart the air malign,
    So strong was the affectionate appeal.

"O living creature gracious and benignant,
    Who visiting goest through the purple air
    Us, who have stained the world incarnadine,[3]   90

If were the King of the Universe our friend,
    We would pray unto him to give thee peace,
    Since thou hast pity on our woe perverse.

Of what it pleases thee to hear and speak,
    That will we hear, and we will speak to you,   95
    While silent is the wind, as it is now.

Sitteth the city,[4] wherein I was born,
    Upon the seashore where the Po descends
    To rest in peace with all his retinue.

Love, that on gentle heart doth swiftly seize,   100
  Seized this man for the person beautiful
  That was ta'en from me, and still the mode offends me.

Love, that exempts no one beloved from loving,
  Seized me with pleasure of this man so strongly,
  That, as thou seest, it doth not yet desert me;   105

Love has conducted us unto one death;
  Caina[5] waiteth him who quenched our life!"
  These words were borne along from them to us.

As soon as I had heard those souls tormented,
  I bowed my face, and so long held it down   110
  Until the Poet said to me: "What thinkest?"

When I made answer, I began: "Alas!
  How many pleasant thoughts, how much desire,
  Conducted these unto the dolorous pass!"

Then unto them I turned me, and I spake,   115
  And I began: "Thine agonies, Francesca,
  Sad and compassionate to weeping make me.

But tell me, at the time of those sweet sighs,
  By what and in what manner Love conceded,
  That you should know your dubious desires?"   120

And she to me: "There is no greater sorrow
  Than to be mindful of the happy time
  In misery, and that thy Teacher knows.

But, if to recognize the earliest root
  Of love in us thou hast so great desire,   125
  I will do even as he who weeps and speaks.

One day we reading were for our delight
    Of Launcelot, how Love did him enthrall.
    Alone we were and without any fear.

Full many a time our eyes together drew   130
    That reading, and drove the color from our faces;
    But one point only was it that o'ercame us.

When as we read of the much-longed-for smile
    Being by such a noble lover kissed,
    This one, who ne'er from me shall be divided,   135

Kissed me upon the mouth all palpitating.
    Galeotto[6] was the book and he who wrote it.
    That day no farther did we read therein."

And all the while one spirit uttered this,
    The other one did weep so, that, for pity,   140
    I swooned away as if I had been dying,

And fell, even as a dead body falls.

⊰ CANTO VI ⊱

The Third Circle: The Gluttonous—Cerberus—
The Eternal Rain—Ciacco—Florence

AT THE RETURN OF CONSCIOUSNESS, THAT CLOSED
Before the pity of those two relations,
Which utterly with sadness had confused me,

New torments I behold, and new tormented
　　Around me, whichsoever way I move,　　　　　　　5
　　And whichsoever way I turn, and gaze.

In the third circle am I of the rain
　　Eternal, maledict, and cold, and heavy;
　　Its law and quality are never new.

Huge hail, and water somber-hued, and snow,　　　10
　　Athwart the tenebrous air pour down amain;
　　Noisome the earth is, that receiveth this.

Cerberus,[1] monster cruel and uncouth,
　　With his three gullets like a dog is barking
　　Over the people that are there submerged.　　　15

Red eyes he has, and unctuous beard and black,
　　And belly large, and armed with claws his hands;
　　He rends the spirits, flays, and quarters them.

Howl the rain maketh them like unto dogs;
    One side they make a shelter for the other;   20
    Oft turn themselves the wretched reprobates.

When Cerberus perceived us, the great worm!
    His mouths he opened, and displayed his tusks;
    Not a limb had he that was motionless.

And my Conductor, with his spans extended,   25
    Took of the earth, and with his fists well filled,
    He threw it into those rapacious gullets.

Such as that dog is, who by barking craves,
    And quiet grows soon as his food he gnaws,
    For to devour it he but thinks and struggles,   30

The like became those muzzles filth-begrimed
    Of Cerberus the demon, who so thunders
    Over the souls that they would fain be deaf.

We passed across the shadows, which subdues
    The heavy rainstorm, and we placed our feet   35
    Upon their vanity that person seems.

They all were lying prone upon the earth,
    Excepting one, who sat upright as soon
    As he beheld us passing on before him.

"O thou that art conducted through this Hell,"   40
    He said to me, "recall me, if thou canst;
    Thyself wast made before I was unmade."

And I to him: "The anguish which thou hast
    Perhaps doth draw thee out of my remembrance,
    So that it seems not I have ever seen thee.   45

But tell me who thou art, that in so doleful
    A place art put, and in such punishment,
    If some are greater, none is so displeasing."

And he to me: "Thy city, which is full
    Of envy so that now the sack runs over,   50
    Held me within it in the life serene.

You citizens were wont to call me Ciacco;[2]
    For the pernicious sin of gluttony
    I, as thou seest, am battered by this rain.

And I, sad soul, am not the only one,   55
    For all these suffer the like penalty
    For the like sin"; and word no more spake he.

I answered him: "Ciacco, thy wretchedness
    Weighs on me so that it to weep invites me;
    But tell me, if thou knowest, to what shall come   60

The citizens of the divided city;
    If any there be just; and the occasion
    Tell me why so much discord has assailed it."

And he to me: "They, after long contention,
    Will come to bloodshed; and the rustic party   65
    Will drive the other out with much offense.

Then afterwards behoves it this one fall
    Within three suns, and rise again the other
    By force of him who now is on the coast.[3]

High will it hold its forehead a long while,   70
    Keeping the other under heavy burdens,
    Howe'er it weeps thereat and is indignant.

The just are two,[4] and are not understood there;
   Envy and Arrogance and Avarice
   Are the three sparks that have all hearts enkindled."   75

Here ended he his tearful utterance;
   And I to him: "I wish thee still to teach me,
   And make a gift to me of further speech.

Farinata and Tegghiaio, once so worthy,
   Jacopo Rusticucci, Arrigo, and Mosca,[5]   80
   And others who on good deeds set their thoughts,

Say where they are, and cause that I may know them;
   For great desire constraineth me to learn
   If Heaven doth sweeten them, or Hell envenom."

And he: "They are among the blacker souls;   85
   A different sin downweighs them to the bottom;
   If thou so far descendest, thou canst see them.

But when thou art again in the sweet world,
   I pray thee to the mind of others bring me;
   No more I tell thee and no more I answer."   90

Then his straightforward eyes he turned askance,
   Eyed me a little, and then bowed his head;
   He fell therewith prone like the other blind.

And the Guide said to me: "He wakes no more
   This side the sound of the angelic trumpet;   95
   When shall approach the hostile Potentate,

Each one shall find again his dismal tomb,
   Shall reassume his flesh and his own figure,
   Shall hear what through eternity re-echoes."

So we passed onward o'er the filthy mixture   100
    Of shadows and of rain with footsteps slow,
    Touching a little on the future life.

Wherefore I said: "Master, these torments here,
    Will they increase after the mighty sentence,
    Or lesser be, or will they be as burning?"   105

And he to me: "Return unto thy science,
    Which wills, that as the thing more perfect is,
    The more it feels of pleasure and of pain.

Albeit that this people maledict
    To true perfection never can attain,   110
    Hereafter more than now they look to be."

Round in a circle by that road we went,
    Speaking much more, which I do not repeat;
    We came unto the point where the descent is;

There we found Plutus the great enemy.   115

⇥ CANTO VII ⇥

The Fourth Circle: The Avaricious and the Prodigal—Plutus—
Fortune and Her Wheel—The Fifth Circle: The Irascible
and the Sullen—Styx

"Papë Satàn, Papë Satàn, Aleppë!"
Thus Plutus[1] with his clucking voice began;
And that benignant Sage, who all things knew,

Said, to encourage me: "Let not thy fear
   Harm thee; for any power that he may have   5
   Shall not prevent thy going down this crag."

Then he turned round unto that bloated lip,
   And said: "Be silent, thou accursed wolf;
   Consume within thyself with thine own rage.

Not causeless is this journey to the abyss;   10
   Thus is it willed on high, where Michael[2] wrought
   Vengeance upon the proud adultery."

Even as the sails inflated by the wind
   Involved together fall when snaps the mast,
   So fell the cruel monster to the earth.   15

Thus we descended into the fourth chasm,
    Gaining still farther on the dolesome shore
    Which all the woe of the universe insacks.

Justice of God, ah! who heaps up so many
    New toils and sufferings as I beheld?   20
    And why doth our transgression waste us so?

As doth the billow there upon Charybdis,[3]
    That breaks itself on that which it encounters,
    So here the folk must dance their roundelay.

Here saw I people, more than elsewhere, many,   25
    On one side and the other, with great howls,
    Rolling weights forward by main force of chest.

They clashed together, and then at that point
    Each one turned backward, rolling retrograde,
    Crying, "Why keepest?" and, "Why squanderest thou?"   30

Thus they returned along the lurid circle
    On either hand unto the opposite point,
    Shouting their shameful meter evermore.

Then each, when he arrived there, wheeled about
    Through his half-circle to another joust;   35
    And I, who had my heart pierced as it were,

Exclaimed: "My Master, now declare to me
    What people these are, and if all were clerks,
    These shaven crowns upon the left of us."

And he to me: "All of them were asquint   40
    In intellect in the first life, so much
    That there with measure they no spending made.

Clearly enough their voices bark it forth,
    Whene'er they reach the two points of the circle,
    Where sunders them the opposite defect.   45

Clerks those were who no hairy covering
    Have on the head, and Popes and Cardinals,
    In whom doth Avarice practice its excess."

And I: "My Master, among such as these
    I ought forsooth to recognize some few,   50
    Who were infected with these maladies."

And he to me: "Vain thought thou entertainest;
    The undiscerning life which made them sordid
    Now makes them unto all discernment dim.

Forever shall they come to these two buttings;   55
    These from the sepulcher shall rise again
    With the fist closed, and these with tresses shorn.

Ill giving and ill keeping the fair world
    Have ta'en from them, and placed them in this scuffle;
    Whate'er it be, no words adorn I for it.   60

Now canst thou, Son, behold the transient farce
    Of goods that are committed unto Fortune,
    For which the human race each other buffet;

For all the gold that is beneath the moon,
    Or ever has been, of these weary souls   65
    Could never make a single one repose."

"Master," I said to him, "now tell me also
    What is this Fortune which thou speakest of,
    That has the world's goods so within its clutches?"

And he to me: "O creatures imbecile,   70
    What ignorance is this which doth beset you?
    Now will I have thee learn my judgment of her.

He whose omniscience everything transcends
    The heavens created, and gave who should guide them,
    That every part to every part may shine,   75

Distributing the light in equal measure;
    He in like manner to the mundane splendors
    Ordained a general ministress and guide,

That she might change at times the empty treasures
    From race to race, from one blood to another,   80
    Beyond resistance of all human wisdom.

Therefore one people triumphs, and another
    Languishes, in pursuance of her judgment,
    Which hidden is, as in the grass a serpent.

Your knowledge has no counterstand against her;   85
    She makes provision, judges, and pursues
    Her governance, as theirs the other gods.

Her permutations have not any truce;
    Necessity makes her precipitate,
    So often cometh who his turn obtains.   90

And this is she who is so crucified
    Even by those who ought to give her praise,
    Giving her blame amiss, and bad repute.

But she is blissful, and she hears it not;
    Among the other primal creatures gladsome   95
    She turns her sphere, and blissful she rejoices.

Let us descend now unto greater woe;
    Already sinks each star that was ascending
    When I set out, and loitering is forbidden."

We crossed the circle to the other bank,   100
    Near to a fount that boils, and pours itself
    Along a gully that runs out of it.

The water was more somber far than perse;
    And we, in company with the dusky waves,
    Made entrance downward by a path uncouth.   105

A marsh it makes, which has the name of Styx,
    This tristful brooklet, when it has descended
    Down to the foot of the malign gray shores.

And I, who stood intent upon beholding,
    Saw people mud-besprent in that lagoon,   110
    All of them naked and with angry look.

They smote each other not alone with hands,
    But with the head and with the breast and feet,
    Tearing each other piecemeal with their teeth.

Said the good Master: "Son, thou now beholdest   115
    The souls of those whom anger overcame;
    And likewise I would have thee know for certain

Beneath the water people are who sigh
    And make this water bubble at the surface,
    As the eye tells thee wheresoe'er it turns.   120

Fixed in the mire they say, 'We sullen were
    In the sweet air, which by the sun is gladdened,
    Bearing within ourselves the sluggish reek;

Now we are sullen in this sable mire.'
    This hymn do they keep gurgling in their throats,   125
    For with unbroken words they cannot say it."

Thus we went circling round the filthy fen
    A great arc 'twixt the dry bank and the swamp,
    With eyes turned unto those who gorge the mire;

Unto the foot of a tower we came at last.   130

⊰ CANTO VIII ⊱

Phlegyas—Philippo Argenti—The Gate of the City of Dis

I SAY, CONTINUING, THAT LONG BEFORE
We to the foot of that high tower had come,
Our eyes went upward to the summit of it,

By reason of two flamelets we saw placed there,
    And from afar another answer them,   5
    So far, that hardly could the eye attain it.

And, to the sea of all discernment turned,
    I said: "What sayeth this, and what respondeth
    That other fire? and who are they that made it?"

And he to me: "Across the turbid waves   10
    What is expected thou canst now discern,
    If reek of the morass conceal it not."

Cord never shot an arrow from itself
    That sped away athwart the air so swift,
    As I beheld a very little boat   15

Come o'er the water tow'rds us at that moment,
    Under the guidance of a single pilot,
    Who shouted, "Now art thou arrived, fell soul?"

"Phlegyas, Phlegyas,[1] thou criest out in vain
    For this once," said my Lord; "thou shalt not have us   20
    Longer than in the passing of the slough."

As he who listens to some great deceit
    That has been done to him, and then resents it,
    Such became Phlegyas, in his gathered wrath.

My Guide descended down into the boat,   25
    And then he made me enter after him,
    And only when I entered seemed it laden.

Soon as the Guide and I were in the boat,
    The antique prow goes on its way, dividing
    More of the water than 'tis wont with others.   30

While we were running through the dead canal,
    Uprose in front of me one full of mire,
    And said, "Who 'rt thou that comest ere the hour?"

And I to him: "Although I come, I stay not;
    But who art thou that hast become so squalid?"   35
    "Thou seest that I am one who weeps," he answered.

And I to him: "With weeping and with wailing,
    Thou spirit maledict, do thou remain;
    For thee I know,[2] though thou art all defiled."

Then stretched he both his hands unto the boat;   40
    Whereat my wary Master thrust him back,
    Saying, "Away there with the other dogs!"

Thereafter with his arms he clasped my neck;
    He kissed my face, and said: "Disdainful soul,
    Blessed be she who bore thee in her bosom.   45

That was an arrogant person in the world;
  Goodness is none, that decks his memory;
  So likewise here his shade is furious.

How many are esteemed great kings up there,
  Who here shall be like unto swine in mire,   50
  Leaving behind them horrible dispraises!"

And I: "My Master, much should I be pleased,
  If I could see him soused into this broth,
  Before we issue forth out of the lake."

And he to me: "Ere unto thee the shore   55
  Reveal itself, thou shalt be satisfied;
  Such a desire 'tis meet thou shouldst enjoy."

A little after that, I saw such havoc
  Made of him by the people of the mire,
  That still I praise and thank my God for it.   60

They all were shouting, "At Philippo Argenti!"
  And that exasperate spirit Florentine
  Turned round upon himself with his own teeth.

We left him there, and more of him I tell not;
  But on mine ears there smote a lamentation,   65
  Whence forward I intent unbar mine eyes.

And the good Master said: "Even now, my Son,
  The city draweth near whose name is Dis,³
  With the grave citizens, with the great throng."

And I: "Its mosques already, Master, clearly   70
  Within there in the valley I discern
  Vermilion, as if issuing from the fire

They were." And he to me: "The fire eternal
    That kindles them within makes them look red,
    As thou beholdest in this nether Hell."   75

Then we arrived within the moats profound,
    That circumvallate that disconsolate city;
    The walls appeared to me to be of iron.

Not without making first a circuit wide,
    We came unto a place where loud the pilot   80
    Cried out to us, "Debark, here is the entrance."

More than a thousand at the gates I saw
    Out of the Heavens rained down, who angrily
    Were saying, "Who is this that without death

Goes through the kingdom of the people dead?"   85
    And my sagacious Master made a sign
    Of wishing secretly to speak with them.

A little then they quelled their great disdain,
    And said: "Come thou alone, and he begone
    Who has so boldly entered these dominions.   90

Let him return alone by his mad road;
    Try, if he can; for thou shalt here remain,
    Who hast escorted him through such dark regions."

Think, Reader, if I was discomforted
    At utterance of the accursed words;   95
    For never to return here I believed.

"O my dear Guide, who more than seven times
    Hast rendered me security, and drawn me
    From imminent peril that before me stood,

Do not desert me," said I, "thus undone;   100
    And if the going farther be denied us,
    Let us retrace our steps together swiftly."

And that Lord, who had led me thitherward,
    Said unto me: "Fear not; because our passage
    None can take from us, it by Such is given.   105

But here await me, and thy weary spirit
    Comfort and nourish with a better hope;
    For in this nether world I will not leave thee."

So onward goes and there abandons me
    My Father sweet, and I remain in doubt,   110
    For No and Yes within my head contend.

I could not hear what he proposed to them;
    But with them there he did not linger long,
    Ere each within in rivalry ran back.

They closed the portals, those our adversaries,   115
    On my Lord's breast, who had remained without
    And turned to me with footsteps far between.

His eyes cast down, his forehead shorn had he
    Of all its boldness, and he said, with sighs,
    "Who has denied to me the dolesome houses?"   120

And unto me: "Thou, because I am angry,
    Fear not, for I will conquer in the trial,
    Whatever for defense within be planned.

This arrogance of theirs is nothing new;
    For once they used it at less secret gate,   125
    Which finds itself without a fastening still.

O'er it didst thou behold the dead inscription;
  And now this side of it descends the steep,
  Passing across the circles without escort,

One by whose means the city shall be opened."   130

⤙ CANTO IX ⤚

The Furies and Medusa—The Angel—The City of Dis—
The Sixth Circle: Heresiarchs

THAT HUE WHICH COWARDICE BROUGHT OUT ON ME,
Beholding my Conductor backward turn,
Sooner repressed within him his new color.

He stopped attentive, like a man who listens,
 Because the eye could not conduct him far   5
 Through the black air, and through the heavy fog.

"Still it behoveth us to win the fight,"
 Began he; "Else . . . Such offered us herself . . .
 O how I long that some one here arrive!"

Well I perceived, as soon as the beginning   10
 He covered up with what came afterward,
 That they were words quite different from the first;

But nonetheless his saying gave me fear,
 Because I carried out the broken phrase,
 Perhaps to a worse meaning than he had.   15

"Into this bottom of the doleful conch
 Doth any e'er descend from the first grade,
 Which for its pain has only hope cut off?"

This question put I; and he answered me:
    "Seldom it comes to pass that one of us   20
    Maketh the journey upon which I go.

True is it, once before I here below
    Was conjured by that pitiless Erictho,[1]
    Who summoned back the shades unto their bodies.

Naked of me short while the flesh had been,   25
    Before within that wall she made me enter,
    To bring a spirit from the circle of Judas;

That is the lowest region and the darkest,
    And farthest from the heaven which circles all.
    Well know I the way; therefore be reassured.   30

This fen, which a prodigious stench exhales,
    Encompasses about the city dolent,
    Where now we cannot enter without anger."

And more he said, but not in mind I have it;
    Because mine eye had altogether drawn me   35
    Tow'rds the high tower with the red-flaming summit,

Where in a moment saw I swift uprisen
    The three infernal Furies stained with blood,
    Who had the limbs of women and their mien,

And with the greenest hydras were begirt;   40
    Small serpents and cerastes were their tresses,
    Wherewith their horrid temples were entwined.

And he who well the handmaids of the Queen
    Of everlasting lamentation knew,
    Said unto me: "Behold the fierce Erinnys."[2]   45

This is Megæra, on the left-hand side;
    She who is weeping on the right, Alecto;
    Tisiphone is between"; and then was silent.

Each one her breast was rending with her nails;
    They beat them with their palms, and cried so loud,   50
    That I for dread pressed close unto the Poet.

"Medusa[3] come, so we to stone will change him!"
    All shouted looking down; "in evil hour
    Avenged we not on Theseus[4] his assault!"

"Turn thyself round, and keep thine eyes close shut,   55
    For if the Gorgon appear, and thou shouldst see it,
    No more returning upward would there be."

Thus said the Master; and he turned me round
    Himself, and trusted not unto my hands
    So far as not to blind me with his own.   60

O ye who have undistempered intellects,
    Observe the doctrine that conceals itself
    Beneath the veil of the mysterious verses!

And now there came across the turbid waves
    The clangor of a sound with terror fraught,   65
    Because of which both of the margins trembled;

Not otherwise it was than of a wind
    Impetuous on account of adverse heats,
    That smites the forest, and, without restraint,

The branches rends, beats down, and bears away;   70
    Right onward, laden with dust, it goes superb,
    And puts to flight the wild beasts and the shepherds.

Mine eyes he loosed, and said: "Direct the nerve
    Of vision now along that ancient foam,
    There yonder where that smoke is most intense."   75

Even as the frogs before the hostile serpent
    Across the water scatter all abroad,
    Until each one is huddled in the earth.

More than a thousand ruined souls I saw,
    Thus fleeing from before one who on foot   80
    Was passing o'er the Styx with soles unwet.

From off his face he fanned that unctuous air,
    Waving his left hand oft in front of him,
    And only with that anguish seemed he weary.

Well I perceived one sent from Heaven[5] was he,   85
    And to the Master turned; and he made sign
    That I should quiet stand, and bow before him.

Ah! how disdainful he appeared to me!
    He reached the gate, and with a little rod
    He opened it, for there was no resistance.   90

"O banished out of Heaven, people despised!"
    Thus he began upon the horrid threshold;
    "Whence is this arrogance within you couched?

Wherefore recalcitrate against that will,
    From which the end can never be cut off,   95
    And which has many times increased your pain?

What helpeth it to butt against the fates?
    Your Cerberus, if you remember well,
    For that still bears his chin and gullet peeled."

Then he returned along the miry road,   100
    And spake no word to us, but had the look
    Of one whom other care constrains and goads

Than that of him who in his presence is;
    And we our feet directed tow'rds the city,
    After those holy words all confident.   105

Within we entered without any contest;
    And I, who inclination had to see
    What the condition such a fortress holds,

Soon as I was within, cast round mine eye,
    And see on every hand an ample plain,   110
    Full of distress and torment terrible.

Even as at Arles, where stagnant grows the Rhone,
    Even as at Pola[6] near to the Quarnaro,
    That shuts in Italy and bathes its borders,

The sepulchers make all the place uneven;   115
    So likewise did they there on every side,
    Saving that there the manner was more bitter;

For flames between the sepulchers were scattered,
    By which they so intensely heated were,
    That iron more so asks not any art.   120

All of their coverings uplifted were,
    And from them issued forth such dire laments,
    Sooth seemed they of the wretched and tormented.

And I: "My Master, what are all those people
    Who, having sepulture within those tombs,   125
    Make themselves audible by doleful sighs?"

And he to me: "Here are the Heresiarchs,
  With their disciples of all sects, and much
  More than thou thinkest laden are the tombs.

Here like together with its like is buried;   130
  And more and less the monuments are heated."
  And when he to the right had turned, we passed

Between the torments and high parapets.

⫷ CANTO X ⫸

Farinata and Cavalcante de' Cavalcanti—
Discourse on the Knowledge of the Damned

NOW ONWARD GOES, ALONG A NARROW PATH
Between the torments and the city wall,
My Master, and I follow at his back.

"O power supreme, that through these impious circles
    Turnest me," I began, "as pleases thee,   5
    Speak to me, and my longings satisfy;

The people who are lying in these tombs,
    Might they be seen? already are uplifted
    The covers all, and no one keepeth guard."

And he to me: "They all will be closed up   10
    When from Jehoshaphat they shall return
    Here with the bodies they have left above.

Their cemetery have upon this side
    With Epicurus all his followers,
    Who with the body mortal make the soul;   15

But in the question thou dost put to me,
    Within here shalt thou soon be satisfied,
    And likewise in the wish thou keepest silent."

And I: "Good Leader, I but keep concealed
 From thee my heart, that I may speak the less,   20
 Nor only now hast thou thereto disposed me."

"O Tuscan, thou who through the city of fire
 Goest alive, thus speaking modestly,
 Be pleased to stay thy footsteps in this place.

Thy mode of speaking makes thee manifest   25
 A native of that noble fatherland,
 To which perhaps I too molestful was."

Upon a sudden issued forth this sound
 From out one of the tombs; wherefore I pressed,
 Fearing, a little nearer to my Leader.   30

And unto me he said: "Turn thee; what dost thou?
 Behold there Farinata[1] who has risen;
 From the waist upwards wholly shalt thou see him."

I had already fixed mine eyes on his,
 And he uprose erect with breast and front   35
 E'en as if Hell he had in great despite.

And with courageous hands and prompt my Leader
 Thrust me between the sepulchers towards him,
 Exclaiming, "Let thy words explicit be."

As soon as I was at the foot of his tomb,   40
 Somewhat he eyed me, and, as if disdainful,
 Then asked of me, "Who were thine ancestors?"

I, who desirous of obeying was,
 Concealed it not, but all revealed to him;
 Whereat he raised his brows a little upward.   45

Then said he: "Fiercely adverse have they been
    To me, and to my fathers, and my party;
    So that two several times I scattered them."

"If they were banished, they returned on all sides,"
    I answered him, "the first time and the second;   50
    But yours have not acquired that art aright."

Then there uprose upon the sight, uncovered
    Down to the chin, a shadow at his side;
    I think that he had risen on his knees.

Round me he gazed, as if solicitude   55
    He had to see if some one else were with me,
    But after his suspicion was all spent,

Weeping, he said to me: "If through this blind
    Prison thou goest by loftiness of genius,
    Where is my son? and why is he not with thee?"   60

And I to him: "I come not of myself;
    He who is waiting yonder leads me here,
    Whom in disdain perhaps your Guido² had."

His language and the mode of punishment
    Already unto me had read his name;   65
    On that account my answer was so full.

Up starting suddenly, he cried out: "How
    Saidst thou—he had? Is he not still alive?
    Does not the sweet light strike upon his eyes?"

When he became aware of some delay,   70
    Which I before my answer made, supine
    He fell again, and forth appeared no more.

But the other, magnanimous, at whose desire
    I had remained, did not his aspect change,
    Neither his neck he moved, nor bent his side.   75

"And if," continuing his first discourse,
    "They have that art," he said, "not learned aright,
    That more tormenteth me, than doth this bed.

But fifty times shall not rekindled be
    The countenance of the Lady who reigns here,   80
    Ere thou shalt know how heavy is that art;

And as thou wouldst to the sweet world return,
    Say why that people is so pitiless
    Against my race in each one of its laws?"

Whence I to him: "The slaughter and great carnage   85
    Which have with crimson stained the Arbia,[3] cause
    Such orisons in our temple to be made."

After his head he with a sigh had shaken,
    "There I was not alone," he said, "nor surely
    Without a cause had with the others moved.   90

But there I was alone, where every one
    Consented to the laying waste of Florence,
    He who defended her with open face."

"Ah! so hereafter may your seed repose,"
    I him entreated, "solve for me that knot,   95
    Which has entangled my conceptions here.

It seems that you can see, if I hear rightly,
    Beforehand whatsoe'er time brings with it,
    And in the present have another mode."

"We see, like those who have imperfect sight,   100
　　The things," he said, "that distant are from us;
　　So much still shines on us the Sovereign Ruler.

When they draw near, or are, is wholly vain
　　Our intellect, and if none brings it to us,
　　Not anything know we of your human state.   105

Hence thou canst understand, that wholly dead
　　Will be our knowledge from the moment when
　　The portal of the future shall be closed."

Then I, as if compunctious for my fault,
　　Said: "Now, then, you will tell that fallen one,   110
　　That still his son is with the living joined.

And if just now, in answering, I was dumb,
　　Tell him I did it because I was thinking
　　Already of the error you have solved me."

And now my Master was recalling me,   115
　　Wherefore more eagerly I prayed the spirit
　　That he would tell me who was with him there.

He said: "With more than a thousand here I lie;
　　Within here is the second Frederick,
　　And the Cardinal,[4] and of the rest I speak not."   120

Thereon he hid himself; and I towards
　　The ancient poet turned my steps, reflecting
　　Upon that saying, which seemed hostile to me.

He moved along; and afterward, thus going,
　　He said to me, "Why art thou so bewildered?"   125
　　And I in his inquiry satisfied him.

"Let memory preserve what thou hast heard
   Against thyself," that Sage commanded me,
   "And now attend here"; and he raised his finger.

"When thou shalt be before the radiance sweet   130
   Of her whose beauteous eyes all things behold,
   From her thou'lt know the journey of thy life."

Unto the left hand then he turned his feet;
   We left the wall, and went towards the middle,
   Along a path that strikes into a valley,   135

Which even up there unpleasant made its stench.

⊰ CANTO XI ⊱

The Broken Rocks—Pope Anastasius—General Description
of the Inferno and Its Divisions

UPON THE MARGIN OF A LOFTY BANK
Which great rocks broken in a circle made,
We came upon a still more cruel throng;

And there, by reason of the horrible
    Excess of stench the deep abyss throws out,   5
    We drew ourselves aside behind the cover

Of a great tomb, whereon I saw a writing,
    Which said: "Pope Anastasius I hold,
    Whom out of the right way Photinus[1] drew."

"Slow it behoveth our descent to be,   10
    So that the sense be first a little used
    To the sad blast, and then we shall not heed it."

The Master thus; and unto him I said,
    "Some compensation find, that the time pass not
    Idly"; and he: "Thou seest I think of that.   15

My son, upon the inside of these rocks,"
    Began he then to say, "are three small circles,
    From grade to grade, like those which thou art leaving.

They all are full of spirits maledict;
    But that hereafter sight alone suffice thee,   20
    Hear how and wherefore they are in constraint.

Of every malice that wins hate in Heaven,
    Injury is the end; and all such end
    Either by force or fraud afflicteth others.

But because fraud is man's peculiar vice,   25
    More it displeases God; and so stand lowest
    The fraudulent, and greater dole assails them.

All the first circle of the Violent is;
    But since force may be used against three persons,
    In three rounds 'tis divided and constructed.   30

To God, to ourselves, and to our neighbor can we
    Use force; I say on them and on their things,
    As thou shalt hear with reason manifest.

A death by violence, and painful wounds,
    Are to our neighbor given; and in his substance   35
    Ruin, and arson, and injurious levies;

Whence homicides, and he who smites unjustly,
    Marauders, and freebooters, the first round
    Tormenteth all in companies diverse.

Man may lay violent hands upon himself   40
    And his own goods; and therefore in the second
    Round must perforce without avail repent

Whoever of your world deprives himself,
    Who games,[2] and dissipates his property,
    And weepeth there, where he should jocund be.   45

Violence can be done the Deity,
 In heart denying and blaspheming Him,
 And by disdaining Nature and her bounty.

And for this reason doth the smallest round
 Seal with its signet Sodom and Cahors,   50
 And who, disdaining God, speaks from the heart.

Fraud, wherewithal is every conscience stung,
 A man may practice upon him who trusts,
 And him who doth no confidence imburse.

This latter mode, it would appear, dissevers   55
 Only the bond of love which Nature makes;
 Wherefore within the second circle nestle

Hypocrisy, flattery, and who deals in magic,
 Falsification, theft, and simony,
 Panders, and barrators,[3] and the like filth.   60

By the other mode, forgotten is that love
 Which Nature makes, and what is after added,
 From which there is a special faith engendered.

Hence in the smallest circle, where the point is
 Of the Universe, upon which Dis is seated,   65
 Whoe'er betrays forever is consumed."

And I: "My Master, clear enough proceeds
 Thy reasoning, and full well distinguishes
 This cavern and the people who possess it.

But tell me, those within the fat lagoon,   70
 Whom the wind drives, and whom the rain doth beat,
 And who encounter with such bitter tongues,

Wherefore are they inside of the red city
    Not punished, if God has them in his wrath,
    And if he has not, wherefore in such fashion?"   75

And unto me he said: "Why wanders so
    Thine intellect from that which it is wont?
    Or, sooth, thy mind where is it elsewhere looking?

Hast thou no recollection of those words
    With which thine Ethics thoroughly discusses   80
    The dispositions three, that Heaven abides not—

Incontinence, and Malice, and insane
    Bestiality? and how Incontinence
    Less God offendeth, and less blame attracts?

If thou regardest this conclusion well,   85
    And to thy mind recallest who they are
    That up outside are undergoing penance,

Clearly wilt thou perceive why from these felons
    They separated are, and why less wroth
    Justice divine doth smite them with its hammer."   90

"O Sun, that healest all distempered vision,
    Thou dost content me so, when thou resolvest,
    That doubting pleases me no less than knowing!

Once more a little backward turn thee," said I,
    "There where thou sayest that usury offends   95
    Goodness divine, and disengage the knot."

"Philosophy," he said, "to him who heeds it,
    Noteth, not only in one place alone,
    After what manner Nature takes her course

From Intellect Divine, and from its art;   100
 And if thy Physics carefully thou notest,
 After not many pages shalt thou find,

That this your art as far as possible
 Follows, as the disciple doth the master;
 So that your art is, as it were, God's grandchild.   105

From these two, if thou bringest to thy mind
 Genesis at the beginning, it behoves
 Mankind to gain their life and to advance;

And since the usurer[4] takes another way,
 Nature herself and in her follower   110
 Disdains he, for elsewhere he puts his hope.

But follow, now, as I would fain go on,
 For quivering are the Fishes on the horizon,
 And the Wain wholly over Caurus[5] lies,

And far beyond there we descend the crag."   115

⊰ CANTO XII ⊱

The Minotaur—The Seventh Circle: The Violent—
The River Phlegethon—The Violent against Their Neighbors—
The Centaurs—Tyrants

THE PLACE WHERE TO DESCEND THE BANK WE CAME
Was alpine, and from what was there, moreover,
Of such a kind that every eye would shun it.

Such as that ruin is which in the flank
    Smote, on this side of Trent, the Adige,[1]   5
    Either by earthquake or by failing stay,

For from the mountain's top, from which it moved,
    Unto the plain the cliff is shattered so,
    Some path 'twould give to him who was above;

Even such was the descent of that ravine,   10
    And on the border of the broken chasm
    The infamy of Crete[2] was stretched along,

Who was conceived in the fictitious cow;
    And when he us beheld, he bit himself,
    Even as one whom anger racks within.   15

My Sage towards him shouted: "Peradventure
    Thou think'st that here may be the Duke of Athens,[3]
    Who in the world above brought death to thee?

Get thee gone, beast, for this one cometh not
    Instructed by thy sister, but he comes   20
    In order to behold your punishments."

As is that bull who breaks loose at the moment
    In which he has received the mortal blow,
    Who cannot walk, but staggers here and there,

The Minotaur beheld I do the like;   25
    And he, the wary, cried: "Run to the passage;
    While he wroth, 'tis well thou shouldst descend."

Thus down we took our way o'er that discharge
    Of stones, which oftentimes did move themselves
    Beneath my feet, from the unwonted burden.   30

Thoughtful I went; and he said: "Thou art thinking
    Perhaps upon this ruin, which is guarded
    By that brute anger which just now I quenched.

Now will I have thee know, the other time
    I here descended to the nether Hell,   35
    This precipice had not yet fallen down.

But truly, if I well discern, a little
    Before His coming who the mighty spoil
    Bore off from Dis, in the supernal[4] circle,

Upon all sides the deep and loathsome valley   40
    Trembled so, that I thought the Universe
    Was thrilled with love, by which there are who think

The world ofttimes converted into chaos;
    And at that moment this primeval crag
      Both here and elsewhere made such overthrow.   45

But fix thine eyes below; for draweth near
    The river of blood, within which boiling is
      Whoe'er by violence doth injure others."

O blind cupidity, O wrath insane,
    That spurs us onward so in our short life,   50
      And in the eternal then so badly steeps us!

I saw an ample moat bent like a bow,
    As one which all the plain encompasses,
      Conformable to what my Guide had said.

And between this and the embankment's foot   55
    Centaurs in file were running, armed with arrows,
      As in the world they used the chase to follow.

Beholding us descend, each one stood still,
    And from the squadron three detached themselves,
      With bows and arrows in advance selected;   60

And from afar one cried: "Unto what torment
    Come ye, who down the hillside are descending?
      Tell us from there; if not, I draw the bow."

My Master said: "Our answer will we make
    To Chiron, near you there; in evil hour,   65
      That will of thine was evermore so hasty."

Then touched he me, and said: "This one is Nessus,
    Who perished for the lovely Dejanira,
      And for himself, himself did vengeance take.

And he in the midst, who at his breast is gazing,   70
    Is the great Chiron, who brought up Achilles;
    That other Pholus[5] is, who was so wrathful.

Thousands and thousands go about the moat
    Shooting with shafts whatever soul emerges
    Out of the blood, more than his crime allots."   75

Near we approached unto those monsters fleet;
    Chiron an arrow took, and with the notch
    Backward upon his jaws he put his beard.

After he had uncovered his great mouth,
    He said to his companions: "Are you aware   80
    That he behind moveth whate'er he touches?

Thus are not wont to do the feet of dead men."
    And my good Guide, who now was at his breast,
    Where the two natures are together joined,

Replied: "Indeed he lives, and thus alone   85
    Me it behoves to show him the dark valley;
    Necessity, and not delight, impels us.

Some one[6] withdrew from singing Halleluja,
    Who unto me committed this new office;
    No thief is he, nor I a thievish spirit.   90

But by that virtue through which I am moving
    My steps along this savage thoroughfare,
    Give us some one of thine, to be with us,

And who may show us where to pass the ford,
    And who may carry this one on his back;   95
    For 'tis no spirit that can walk the air."

Upon his right breast Chiron wheeled about,
    And said to Nessus: "Turn and do thou guide them,
    And warn aside, if other band may meet you."

We with our faithful escort onward moved   100
    Along the brink of the vermilion boiling,
    Wherein the boiled were uttering loud laments.

People I saw within up to the eyebrows,
    And the great Centaur said: "Tyrants are these,
    Who dealt in bloodshed and in pillaging.   105

Here they lament their pitiless mischiefs; here
    Is Alexander, and fierce Dionysius[7]
    Who upon Sicily brought dolorous years.

That forehead there which has the hair so black
    Is Azzolin;[8] and the other who is blond,   110
    Obizzo[9] is of Esti, who, in truth,

Up in the world was by his stepson slain."
    Then turned I to the Poet; and he said,
    "Now he be first to thee, and second I."

A little farther on the Centaur stopped   115
    Above a folk, who far down as the throat
    Seemed from that boiling stream to issue forth.

A shade he showed us on one side alone,
    Saying: "He cleft asunder in God's bosom
    The heart that still upon the Thames is honored."[10]   120

Then people saw I, who from out the river
    Lifted their heads and also all the chest;
    And many among these I recognized.

Thus ever more and more grew shallower
    That blood, so that the feet alone it covered;   125
    And there across the moat our passage was.

"Even as thou here upon this side beholdest
    The boiling stream, that aye diminishes,"
    The Centaur said, "I wish thee to believe

That on this other more and more declines   130
    Its bed, until it reunites itself
    Where it behoveth tyranny to groan.

Justice divine, upon this side, is goading
    That Attila, who was a scourge on earth,
    And Pyrrhus, and Sextus; and forever milks   135

The tears which with the boiling it unseals
    In Rinier da Corneto and Rinier Pazzo,[11]
    Who made upon the highways so much war."

Then back he turned, and passed again the ford.

\dashuparrow CANTO XIII \dashdownarrow

The Wood of Thorns—The Harpies—The Violent against Themselves—
Suicides—Pier della Vigna—Lano and Jacopo da Sant' Andrea

NOT YET HAD NESSUS REACHED THE OTHER SIDE,
When we had put ourselves within a wood,
That was not marked by any path whatever.

Not foliage green, but of a dusky color,
   Not branches smooth, but gnarled and intertangled,   5
   Not appletrees were there, but thorns with poison.

Such tangled thickets have not, nor so dense,
   Those savage wild beasts, that in hatred hold
   'Twixt Cecina and Corneto[1] the tilled places.

There do the hideous Harpies[2] make their nests,   10
   Who chased the Trojans from the Strophades,
   With sad announcement of impending doom;

Broad wings have they, and necks and faces human,
   And feet with claws, and their great bellies fledged;
   They make laments upon the wondrous trees.   15

And the good Master: "Ere thou enter farther,
   Know that thou art within the second round,"
   Thus he began to say, "and shalt be, till

Thou comest out upon the horrible sand;
    Therefore look well around, and thou shalt see   20
    Things that will credence give unto my speech."

I heard on all sides lamentations uttered,
    And person none beheld I who might make them,
    Whence, utterly bewildered, I stood still.

I think he thought that I perhaps might think   25
    So many voices issued through those trunks
    From people who concealed themselves from us;

Therefore the Master said: "If thou break off
    Some little spray from any of these trees,
    The thoughts thou hast will wholly be made vain."   30

Then stretched I forth my hand a little forward,
    And plucked a branchlet off from a great thorn;
    And the trunk cried, "Why dost thou mangle me?"

After it had become embrowned with blood,
    It recommenced its cry: "Why dost thou rend me?   35
    Hast thou no spirit of pity whatsoever?

Men once we were, and now are changed to trees;
    Indeed, thy hand should be more pitiful,
    Even if the souls of serpents we had been."

As out of a green brand, that is on fire   40
    At one of the ends, and from the other drips
    And hisses with the wind that is escaping;

So from that splinter issued forth together
    Both words and blood; whereat I let the tip
    Fall, and stood like a man who is afraid.   45

"Had he been able sooner to believe,"
    My Sage made answer, "O thou wounded soul,
    What only in my verses he has seen,

Not upon thee had he stretched forth his hand;
    Whereas the thing incredible has caused me   50
    To put him to an act which grieveth me.

But tell him who thou wast, so that by way
    Of some amends thy fame he may refresh
    Up in the world, to which he can return."

And the trunk said: "So thy sweet words allure me,   55
    I cannot silent be; and you be vexed not,
    That I a little to discourse am tempted.

I am the one who both keys had in keeping[3]
    Of Frederick's heart, and turned them to and fro
    So softly in unlocking and in locking,   60

That from his secrets most men I withheld;
    Fidelity I bore the glorious office
    So great, I lost thereby my sleep and pulses.

The courtesan who never from the dwelling
    Of Cæsar turned aside her strumpet eyes,   65
    Death universal and the vice of courts,

Inflamed against me all the other minds,
    And they, inflamed, did so inflame Augustus,[4]
    That my glad honors turned to dismal mournings.

My spirit, in disdainful exultation,   70
    Thinking by dying to escape disdain,
    Made me unjust against myself, the just.

I, by the roots unwonted of this wood,
    Do swear to you that never broke I faith
    Unto my lord, who was so worthy of honor;   75

And to the world if one of you return,
    Let him my memory comfort, which is lying
    Still prostrate from the blow that envy dealt it."

Waited awhile, and then: "Since he is silent,"
    The Poet said to me, "lose not the time,   80
    But speak, and question him, if more may please thee."

Whence I to him: "Do thou again inquire
    Concerning what thou thinks't will satisfy me;
    For I cannot, such pity is in my heart."

Therefore he recommenced: "So may the man   85
    Do for thee freely what thy speech implores,
    Spirit incarcerate, again be pleased

To tell us in what way the soul is bound
    Within these knots; and tell us, if thou canst,
    If any from such members e'er is freed."   90

Then blew the trunk amain, and afterward
    The wind was into such a voice converted:
    "With brevity shall be replied to you.

When the exasperated soul abandons
    The body whence it rent itself away,   95
    Minos consigns it to the seventh abyss.

It falls into the forest, and no part
    Is chosen for it; but where Fortune hurls it,
    There like a grain of spelt it germinates.

It springs a sapling, and a forest tree;   100
    The Harpies, feeding then upon its leaves,
    Do pain create, and for the pain an outlet.

Like others for our spoils shall we return;
    But not that any one may them revest,
    For 'tis not just to have what one casts off.   105

Here we shall drag them, and along the dismal
    Forest our bodies shall suspended be,
    Each to the thorn of his molested shade."

We were attentive still unto the trunk,
    Thinking that more it yet might wish to tell us,   110
    When by a tumult we were overtaken,

In the same way as he is who perceives
    The boar and chase approaching to his stand,
    Who hears the crashing of the beasts and branches;

And two behold! upon our left-hand side,   115
    Naked and scratched, fleeing so furiously,
    That of the forest every fan they broke.

He who was in advance: "Now help, Death, help!"
    And the other one, who seemed to lag too much,
    Was shouting: "Lano, were not so alert   120

Those legs of thine at joustings of the Toppo!"
    And then, perchance because his breath was failing,
    He grouped himself together with a bush.

Behind them was the forest full of black
    She-mastiffs, ravenous, and swift of foot   125
    As greyhounds, who are issuing from the chain.

On him who had crouched down they set their teeth,
    And him they lacerated piece by piece,
    Thereafter bore away those aching members.

Thereat my Escort took me by the hand,   130
    And led me to the bush, that all in vain
    Was weeping from its bloody lacerations.

"O Jacopo,"[5] it said, "of Sant' Andrea,
    What helped it thee of me to make a screen?
    What blame have I in thy nefarious life?"   135

When near him had the Master stayed his steps,
    He said: "Who wast thou, that through wounds so many[6]
    Art blowing out with blood thy dolorous speech?"

And he to us: "O souls, that hither come
    To look upon the shameful massacre   140
    That has so rent away from me my leaves,

Gather them up beneath the dismal bush;
    I of that city was which to the Baptist
    Changed its first patron, wherefore he for this

Forever with his art will make it sad.   145
    And were it not that on the pass of Arno
    Some glimpses of him are remaining still,

Those citizens, who afterwards rebuilt it
    Upon the ashes left by Attila,[7]
    In vain had caused their labor to be done.   150

Of my own house I made myself a gibbet."

⊰ CANTO XIV ⊱

The Sand Waste and the Rain of Fire—The Violent against God—
Capaneus—The Statue of Time, and the Four Infernal Rivers

BECAUSE THE CHARITY OF MY NATIVE PLACE
Constrained me, gathered I the scattered leaves,
And gave them back to him, who now was hoarse.

Then came we to the confine, where disparted
    The second round is from the third, and where   5
    A horrible form of Justice is beheld.

Clearly to manifest these novel things,
    I say that we arrived upon a plain,
    Which from its bed rejecteth every plant;

The dolorous forest is a garland to it   10
    All round about, as the sad moat to that;
    There close upon the edge we stayed our feet.

The soil was of an arid and thick sand,
    Not of another fashion made than that
    Which by the feet of Cato[1] once was pressed.   15

Vengeance of God, O how much oughtest thou
    By each one to be dreaded, who doth read
    That which was manifest unto mine eyes!

Of naked souls beheld I many herds,
    Who all were weeping very miserably,   20
    And over them seemed set a law diverse.

Supine upon the ground some folk were lying;
    And some were sitting all drawn up together,
    And others went about continually.

Those who were going round were far the more,   25
    And those were less who lay down to their torment,
    But had their tongues more loosed to lamentation.

O'er all the sand-waste, with a gradual fall,
    Were raining down dilated flakes of fire,
    As of the snow on Alp without a wind.   30

As Alexander, in those torrid parts
    Of India,[2] beheld upon his host
    Flames fall unbroken till they reached the ground.

Whence he provided with his phalanxes
    To trample down the soil, because the vapor   35
    Better extinguished was while it was single;

Thus was descending the eternal heat,
    Whereby the sand was set on fire, like tinder
    Beneath the steel, for doubling of the dole.

Without repose forever was the dance   40
    Of miserable hands, now there, now here,
    Shaking away from off them the fresh gleeds.[3]

"Master," began I, "thou who overcomest
    All things except the demons dire, that issued
    Against us at the entrance of the gate,   45

Who is that mighty one who seems to heed not
    The fire, and lieth lowering and disdainful,
    So that the rain seems not to ripen him?"

And he himself, who had become aware
    That I was questioning my Guide about him,   50
    Cried: "Such as I was living, am I, dead.

If Jove should weary out his smith, from whom
    He seized in anger the sharp thunderbolt,
    Wherewith upon the last day I was smitten,

And if he wearied out by turns the others   55
    In Mongibello at the swarthy forge,
    Vociferating, 'Help, good Vulcan, help!'

Even as he did there at the fight of Phlegra,[4]
    And shot his bolts at me with all his might,
    He would not have thereby a joyous vengeance."   60

Then did my Leader speak with such great force,
    That I had never heard him speak so loud:
    "O Capaneus, in that is not extinguished

Thine arrogance, thou punished art the more;
    Not any torment, saving thine own rage,   65
    Would be unto thy fury pain complete."

Then he turned round to me with better lip,
    Saying: "One of the Seven Kings was he[5]
    Who Thebes besieged, and held, and seems to hold

God in disdain, and little seems to prize him;   70
    But, as I said to him, his own despites
    Are for his breast the fittest ornaments.

Now follow me, and mind thou do not place
    As yet thy feet upon the burning sand,
    But always keep them close unto the wood."   75

Speaking no word, we came to where there gushes
    Forth from the wood a little rivulet,
    Whose redness makes my hair still stand on end.

As from the Bulicamë[6] springs the brooklet,
    The sinful women later share among them,   80
    So downward through the sand it went its way.

The bottom of it, and both sloping banks,
    Were made of stone, and the margins at the side;
    Whence I perceived that there the passage was.

"In all the rest which I have shown to thee   85
    Since we have entered in within the gate
    Whose threshold unto no one is denied,

Nothing has been discovered by thine eyes
    So notable as is the present river,
    Which all the little flames above it quenches."   90

These words were of my Leader; whence I prayed him
    That he would give me largess of the food,
    For which he had given me largess of desire.

"In the mid-sea there sits a wasted land,"
    Said he thereafterward, "whose name is Crete,   95
    Under whose king[7] the world of old was chaste.

There is a mountain there, that once was glad
    With waters and with leaves, which was called Ida;
    Now 'tis deserted, as a thing worn out.

Rhea[8] once chose it for the faithful cradle   100
    Of her own son; and to conceal him better,
    Whene'er he cried, she there had clamors made.

A grand old man[9] stands in the mount erect,
    Who holds his shoulders turned tow'rds Damietta,
    And looks at Rome as if it were his mirror.   105

His head is fashioned of refined gold,
    And of pure silver are the arms and breast;
    Then he is brass as far down as the fork.

From that point downward all is chosen iron,
    Save that the right foot is of kiln-baked clay,   110
    And more he stands on that than on the other.

Each part, except the gold, is by a fissure
    Asunder cleft, that dripping is with tears,
    Which gathered together perforate that cavern.

From rock to rock they fall into this valley;   115
    Acheron, Styx, and Phlegethon they form;
    Then downward go along this narrow sluice

Unto that point where is no more descending.
    They form Cocytus;[10] what that pool may be
    Thou shalt behold, so here 'tis not narrated."   120

And I to him: "If so the present runnel
    Doth take its rise in this way from our world,
    Why only on this verge appears it to us?"

And he to me: "Thou knowest the place is round,
    And notwithstanding thou hast journeyed far,   125
    Still to the left descending to the bottom,

Thou hast not yet through all the circle turned.
    Therefore if something new appear to us,
    It should not bring amazement to thy face."

And I again: "Master, where shall be found   130
    Lethe and Phlegethon,[11] for of one thou'rt silent,
    And sayest the other of this rain is made?"

"In all thy questions truly thou dost please me,"
    Replied he; "but the boiling of the red
    Water might well solve one of them thou makest.   135

Thou shalt see Lethe, but outside this moat,
    There where the souls repair to lave themselves,
    When sin repented of has been removed."

Then said he: "It is time now to abandon
    The wood; take heed that thou come after me;   140
    A way the margins make that are not burning,

And over them all vapors are extinguished."

⤙ CANTO XV ⤚

The Violent against Nature—Brunetto Latini

NOW BEARS US ONWARD ONE OF THE HARD MARGINS,
And so the brooklet's mist o'ershadows it,
From fire it saves the water and the dikes.

Even as the Flemings, 'twixt Cadsand and Bruges,
    Fearing the flood that tow'rds them hurls itself,   5
    Their bulwarks build to put the sea to flight;

And as the Paduans along the Brenta,
    To guard their villas and their villages,
    Or ever Chiarentana¹ feel the heat;

In such similitude had those been made,   10
    Albeit not so lofty nor so thick,
    Whoever he might be, the master made them.

Now were we from the forest so remote,
    I could not have discovered where it was,
    Even if backward I had turned myself,   15

When we a company of souls encountered,
    Who came beside the dike, and every one
    Gazed at us, as at evening we are wont

83

To eye each other under a new moon,
    And so towards us sharpened they their brows   20
    As an old tailor at the needle's eye.

Thus scrutinized by such a family,
    By some one I was recognized, who seized
    My garment's hem, and cried out, "What a marvel!"

And I, when he stretched forth his arm to me,   25
    On his baked aspect fastened so mine eyes,
    That the scorched countenance prevented not

His recognition by my intellect;
    And bowing down my face unto his own,
    I made reply, "Are you here, Ser Brunetto?"[2]   30

And he: "May't not displease thee, O my son,
    If a brief space with thee Brunetto Latini
    Backward return and let the trail go on."

I said to him: "With all my power I ask it;
    And if you wish me to sit down with you,   35
    I will, if he please, for I go with him."

"O son," he said, "whoever of this herd
    A moment stops, lies then a hundred years,
    Nor fans himself when smiteth him the fire.

Therefore go on; I at thy skirts will come,   40
    And afterward will I rejoin my band,
    Which goes lamenting its eternal doom."

I did not dare to go down from the road
    Level to walk with him; but my head bowed
    I held as one who goeth reverently.   45

And he began: "What fortune or what fate
   Before the last day leadeth thee down here?
   And who is this that showeth thee the way?"

"Up there above us in the life serene,"
   I answered him, "I lost me in a valley,   50
   Or ever yet my age had been completed.

But yestermorn I turned my back upon it;
   This one appeared to me, returning thither,
   And homeward leadeth me along this road."

And he to me: "If thou thy star do follow,   55
   Thou canst not fail thee of a glorious port,
   If well I judged in the life beautiful.

And if I had not died so prematurely,
   Seeing Heaven thus benignant unto thee,
   I would have given thee comfort in the work.   60

But that ungrateful and malignant people,
   Which of old time from Fesole[3] descended,
   And smacks still of the mountain and the granite,

Will make itself, for thy good deeds, thy foe;
   And it is right; for among crabbed sorbs[4]   65
   It ill befits the sweet fig to bear fruit.

Old rumor in the world proclaims them blind;
   A people avaricious, envious, proud;
   Take heed that of their customs thou do cleanse thee.

Thy fortune so much honor doth reserve thee,   70
   One party and the other shall be hungry
   For thee; but far from goat shall be the grass.

Their litter let the beasts of Fesole
　　Make of themselves, nor let them touch the plant,
　　If any still upon their dunghill rise,　　　　　　　　75

In which may yet revive the consecrated
　　Seed of those Romans, who remained there when
　　The nest of such great malice it became."

"If my entreaty wholly were fulfilled,"
　　Replied I to him, "not yet would you be　　　　　　80
　　In banishment from human nature placed;

For in my mind is fixed, and touches now
　　My heart the dear and good paternal image
　　Of you, when in the world from hour to hour

You taught me how a man becomes eternal;　　　　　85
　　And how much I am grateful, while I live
　　Behoves that in my language be discerned.

What you narrate of my career I write,
　　And keep it to be glossed with other text
　　By a Lady who can do it, if I reach her.　　　　　　90

This much will I have manifest to you;
　　Provided that my conscience do not chide me,
　　For whatsoever Fortune I am ready.

Such handsel is not new unto mine ears;
　　Therefore let Fortune turn her wheel around　　　95
　　As it may please her, and the churl his mattock."

My Master thereupon on his right cheek
　　Did backward turn himself, and looked at me;
　　Then said: "He listeneth well who noteth it."

Nor speaking less on that account, I go   100
    With Ser Brunetto, and I ask who are
    His most known and most eminent companions.

And he to me: "To know of some is well;
    Of others it were laudable to be silent,
    For short would be the time for so much speech.   105

Know them in sum, that all of them were clerks,
    And men of letters great and of great fame,
    In the world tainted with the selfsame sin.

Priscian goes yonder with that wretched crowd,
    And Francis of Accorso;[5] and thou hadst seen there,   110
    If thou hadst had a hankering for such scurf,

That one, who by the Servant of the Servants
    From Arno was transferred to Bacchiglione,[6]
    Where he has left his sin-excited nerves.

More would I say, but coming and discoursing   115
    Can be no longer; for that I behold
    New smoke uprising yonder from the sand.

A people comes with whom I may not be;
    Commended unto thee be my Tesoro,[7]
    In which I still live, and no more I ask."   120

Then he turned round, and seemed to be of those
    Who at Verona run for the Green Mantle[8]
    Across the plain; and seemed to be among them

The one who wins, and not the one who loses.

⊰ CANTO XVI ⊱

Guidoguerra, Aldobrandi, and Rusticucci—
Cataract of the River of Blood

NOW WAS I WHERE WAS HEARD THE REVERBERATION
Of water falling into the next round,
Like to that humming which the beehives make,

When shadows three together started forth,
    Running, from out a company that passed   5
    Beneath the rain of the sharp martyrdom.

Towards us came they, and each one cried out:
    "Stop, thou; for by thy garb to us thou seemest
    To be some one of our depraved city."

Ah me! what wounds I saw upon their limbs,   10
    Recent and ancient by the flames burnt in!
    It pains me still but to remember it.

Unto their cries my Teacher paused attentive;
    He turned his face towards me, and "Now wait,"
    He said; "to these we should be courteous.   15

And if it were not for the fire that darts
    The nature of this region, I should say
    That haste were more becoming thee than them."

As soon as we stood still, they recommenced
    The old refrain, and when they overtook us,   20
    Formed of themselves a wheel, all three of them.

As champions stripped and oiled are wont to do,
    Watching for their advantage and their hold,
    Before they come to blows and thrusts between them,

Thus, wheeling round, did every one his visage   25
    Direct to me, so that in opposite wise
    His neck and feet continual journey made.

And, "If the misery of this soft place
    Bring in disdain ourselves and our entreaties,"
    Began one, "and our aspect black and blistered,   30

Let the renown of us thy mind incline
    To tell us who thou art, who thus securely
    Thy living feet dost move along through Hell.

He in whose footprints thou dost see me treading,
    Naked and skinless though he now may go,   35
    Was of a greater rank than thou dost think;

He was the grandson of the good Gualdrada;
    His name was Guidoguerra, and in life
    Much did he with his wisdom and his sword.[1]

The other, who close by me treads the sand,   40
    Tegghiaio Aldobrandi[2] is, whose fame
    Above there in the world should welcome be.

And I, who with them on the cross am placed,
    Jacopo Rusticucci[3] was; and truly
    My savage wife, more than aught else, doth harm me." 45

Could I have been protected from the fire,
    Below I should have thrown myself among them,
    And think the Teacher would have suffered it;

But as I should have burned and baked myself,
    My terror overmastered my good will,   50
    Which made me greedy of embracing them.

Then I began: "Sorrow and not disdain
    Did your condition fix within me so,
    That tardily it wholly is stripped off,

As soon as this my Lord said unto me   55
    Words, on account of which I thought within me
    That people such as you are were approaching.

I of your city am; and evermore
    Your labors and your honorable names
    I with affection have retraced and heard.   60

I leave the gall, and go for the sweet fruits
    Promised to me by the veracious Leader;
    But to the center first I needs must plunge."

"So may the soul for a long while conduct
    Those limbs of thine," did he make answer then, 65
    "And so may thy renown shine after thee,

Valor and courtesy, say if they dwell
    Within our city, as they used to do,
    Or if they wholly have gone out of it;

For Guglielmo Borsier,[4] who is in torment   70
    With us of late, and goes there with his comrades,
    Doth greatly mortify us with his words."

"The new inhabitants and the sudden gains,
    Pride and extravagance have in thee engendered,
    Florence, so that thou weep'st thereat already!"   75

In this wise I exclaimed with face uplifted;
    And the three, taking that for my reply,
    Looked at each other, as one looks at truth.

"If other times so little it doth cost thee,"
    Replied they all, "to satisfy another,   80
    Happy art thou, thus speaking at thy will!

Therefore, if thou escape from these dark places,
    And come to rebehold the beauteous stars,
    When it shall pleasure thee to say, 'I was,'

See that thou speak of us unto the people."   85
    Then they broke up the wheel, and in their flight
    It seemed as if their agile legs were wings.

Not an Amen could possibly be said
    So rapidly as they had disappeared;
    Wherefore the Master deemed best to depart.   90

I followed him, and little had we gone,
    Before the sound of water was so near us,
    That speaking we should hardly have been heard.

Even as that stream which holdeth its own course
    The first from Monte Veso tow'rds the East,   95
    Upon the left-hand slope of Apennine,

Which is above called Acquacheta, ere
 It down descendeth into its low bed,
 And at Forlì is vacant of that name,

Reverberates there above San Benedetto[5]   100
 From Alps, by falling at a single leap,
 Where for a thousand there were room enough;

Thus downward from a bank precipitate,
 We found resounding that dark-tinted water,
 So that it soon the ear would have offended.   105

I had a cord around about me girt,
 And therewithal I whilom had designed
 To take the panther[6] with the painted skin.

After I this had all from me unloosed,
 As my Conductor had commanded me,   110
 I reached it to him, gathered up and coiled,

Whereat he turned himself to the right side,
 And at a little distance from the verge,
 He cast it down into that deep abyss.

"It must needs be some novelty respond,"   115
 I said within myself, "to the new signal
 The Master with his eye is following so."

Ah me! how very cautious men should be
 With those who not alone behold the act,
 But with their wisdom look into the thoughts! 120

He said to me: "Soon there will upward come
 What I await; and what thy thought is dreaming
 Must soon reveal itself unto thy sight."

Aye to that truth which has the face of falsehood,
 A man should close his lips as far as may be,   125
 Because without his fault it causes shame;

But here I cannot; and, Reader, by the notes
 Of this my Comedy to thee I swear,
 So may they not be void of lasting favor,

Athwart that dense and darksome atmosphere   130
 I saw a figure swimming upward come,
 Marvelous unto every steadfast heart,

Even as he returns who goeth down
 Sometimes to clear an anchor, which has grappled
 Reef, or aught else that in the sea is hidden,   135

Who upward stretches, and draws in his feet.

⊰ CANTO XVII ⊱

Geryon—The Violent against Art—Usurers—
Descent into the Abyss of Malebolge

"BEHOLD THE MONSTER WITH THE POINTED TAIL,[1]
Who cleaves the hills, and breaketh walls and weapons,
Behold him who infecteth all the world."

Thus unto me my Guide began to say,
    And beckoned him that he should come to shore,   5
    Near to the confine of the trodden marble;

And that uncleanly image of deceit
    Came up and thrust ashore its head and bust,
    But on the border did not drag its tail.

The face was as the face of a just man,   10
    Its semblance outwardly was so benign,
    And of a serpent all the trunk beside.

Two paws it had, hairy unto the armpits;
    The back, and breast, and both the sides it had
    Depicted o'er with nooses and with shields.   15

With colors more, groundwork or broidery
    Never in cloth did Tartars make nor Turks,
    Nor were such tissues by Arachne laid.

As sometimes wherries lie upon the shore,
    That part are in the water, part on land;   20
    And as among the guzzling Germans there,

The beaver plants himself to wage his war;
    So that vile monster lay upon the border,
    Which is of stone, and shutteth in the sand.

His tail was wholly quivering in the void,   25
    Contorting upwards the envenomed fork,
    That in the guise of scorpion armed its point.

The Guide said: "Now perforce must turn aside
    Our way a little, even to that beast
    Malevolent, that yonder coucheth him."   30

We therefore on the right side descended,
    And made ten steps upon the outer verge,
    Completely to avoid the sand and flame;

And after we are come to him, I see
    A little farther off upon the sand   35
    A people sitting near the hollow place.

Then said to me the Master: "So that full
    Experience of this round thou bear away,
    Now go and see what their condition is.

There let thy conversation be concise;   40
    Till thou returnest I will speak with him,
    That he concede to us his stalwart shoulders."

Thus farther still upon the outermost
   Head of that seventh circle all alone
   I went, where sat the melancholy folk.   45

Out of their eyes was gushing forth their woe;
   This way, that way, they helped them with their hands
   Now from the flames and now from the hot soil.

Not otherwise in summer do the dogs,
   Now with the foot, now with the muzzle, when   50
   By fleas, or flies, or gadflies, they are bitten.

When I had turned mine eyes upon the faces
   Of some, on whom the dolorous fire is falling,
   Not one of them I knew; but I perceived

That from the neck of each there hung a pouch,   55
   Which certain color had, and certain blazon;
   And thereupon it seems their eyes are feeding.

And as I gazing round me come among them,
   Upon a yellow pouch I azure saw
   That had the face and posture of a lion.   60

Proceeding then the current of my sight,
   Another of them saw I, red as blood,
   Display a goose[2] more white than butter is.

And one, who with an azure sow and gravid[3]
   Emblazoned had his little pouch of white,   65
   Said unto me: "What dost thou in this moat?

Now get thee gone; and since thou'rt still alive,
   Know that a neighbor of mine, Vitaliano,
   Will have his seat here on my left-hand side.

A Paduan am I with these Florentines;   70
   Full many a time they thunder in mine ears,
   Exclaiming, 'Come the sovereign cavalier,

He who shall bring the satchel with three goats' ";
   Then twisted he his mouth, and forth he thrust
   His tongue, like to an ox that licks its nose.   75

And fearing lest my longer stay might vex
   Him who had warned me not to tarry long,
   Backward I turned me from those weary souls.

I found my Guide, who had already mounted
   Upon the back of that wild animal,   80
   And said to me: "Now be both strong and bold.

Now we descend by stairways such as these;
   Mount thou in front, for I will be midway,
   So that the tail may have no power to harm thee."

Such as he is who has so near the ague   85
   Of quartan[4] that his nails are blue already,
   And trembles all, but looking at the shade;

Even such became I at those proffered words;
   But shame in me his menaces produced,
   Which maketh servant strong before good master.   90

I seated me upon those monstrous shoulders;
   I wished to say, and yet the voice came not
   As I believed, "Take heed that thou embrace me."

But he, who other times had rescued me
   In other peril, soon as I had mounted,   95
   Within his arms encircled and sustained me,

And said: "Now, Geryon, bestir thyself;
    The circles large, and the descent be little;
    Think of the novel burden which thou hast."

Even as the little vessel shoves from shore,   100
    Backward, still backward, so he thence withdrew;
    And when he wholly felt himself afloat,

There where his breast had been he turned his tail,
    And that extended like an eel he moved,
    And with his paws drew to himself the air.   105

A greater fear I do not think there was
    What time abandoned Phaeton[5] the reins,
    Whereby the heavens, as still appears, were scorched;

Nor when the wretched Icarus[6] his flanks
    Felt stripped of feathers by the melting wax,   110
    His father crying, "An ill way thou takest!"

Than was my own, when I perceived myself
    On all sides in the air, and saw extinguished
    The sight of everything but of the monster.

Onward he goeth, swimming slowly, slowly;   115
    Wheels and descends, but I perceive it only
    By wind upon my face and from below.

I heard already on the right the whirlpool
    Making a horrible crashing under us;
    Whence I thrust out my head with eyes cast downward.   120

Then was I still more fearful of the abyss;
    Because I fires beheld, and heard laments,
    Whereat I, trembling, all the closer cling.

I saw then, for before I had not seen it,
    The turning and descending, by great horrors   125
    That were approaching upon divers sides.

As falcon who has long been on the wing,
    Who, without seeing either lure or bird,
    Maketh the falconer say, "Ah me, thou stoopest,"

Descendeth weary, whence he started swiftly,   130
    Thorough a hundred circles, and alights
    Far from his master, sullen and disdainful;

Even thus did Geryon place us on the bottom,
    Close to the bases of the rough-hewn rock,
    And being disencumbered of our persons,   135

He sped away as arrow from the string.

⚔ CANTO XVIII ⚔

The Eighth Circle, Malebolge: The Fraudulent and the Malicious—
The First Bolgia: Seducers and Panders—Venedico Caccianimico—
Jason—The Second Bolgia: Flatterers—Allessio Interminei—Thais

THERE IS A PLACE IN HELL CALLED MALEBOLGE,[1]
Wholly of stone and of an iron color,
As is the circle that around it turns.

Right in the middle of the field malign
    There yawns a well exceeding wide and deep,   5
    Of which its place the structure will recount.

Round, then, is that enclosure which remains
    Between the well and foot of the high, hard bank,
    And has distinct in valleys ten its bottom.

As where for the protection of the walls   10
    Many and many moats surround the castles,
    The part in which they are a figure forms,

Just such an image those presented there;
    And as about such strongholds from their gates
    Unto the outer bank are little bridges,   15

So from the precipice's base did crags
   Project, which intersected dikes and moats,
   Unto the well that truncates and collects them.

Within this place, down shaken from the back
   Of Geryon, we found us; and the Poet   20
   Held to the left, and I moved on behind.

Upon my right hand I beheld new anguish,
   New torments, and new wielders of the lash,
   Wherewith the foremost Bolgia² was replete.

Down at the bottom were the sinners naked;   25
   This side the middle came they facing us,
   Beyond it, with us, but with greater steps;

Even as the Romans, for the mighty host,
   The year of Jubilee,³ upon the bridge,
   Have chosen a mode to pass the people over;   30

For all upon one side towards the Castle
   Their faces have, and go unto Saint Peter's;
   On the other side they go towards the Mountain.

This side and that, along the livid stone
   Beheld I hornëd demons with great scourges,   35
   Who cruelly were beating them behind.

Ah me! how they did make them lift their legs
   At the first blows! and sooth not any one
   The second waited for, nor for the third.

While I was going on, mine eyes by one   40
   Encountered were; and straight I said: "Already
   With sight of this one I am not unfed."

Therefore I stayed my feet to make him out,
    And with me the sweet Guide came to a stand,
    And to my going somewhat back assented;   45

And he, the scourged one, thought to hide himself,
    Lowering his face, but little it availed him;
    For said I: "Thou that castest down thine eyes,

If false are not the features which thou bearest,
    Thou art Venedico Caccianimico;   50
    But what doth bring thee to such pungent sauces?"[4]

And he to me: "Unwillingly I tell it;
    But forces me thine utterance distinct,
    Which makes me recollect the ancient world.

I was the one who the fair Ghisola   55
    Induced to grant the wishes of the Marquis,
    Howe'er the shameless story may be told.

Not the sole Bolognese am I who weeps here;
    Nay, rather is this place so full of them,
    That not so many tongues today are taught   60

'Twixt Reno and Savena to say *sipa*;
    And if thereof thou wishest pledge or proof,
    Bring to thy mind our avaricious heart."

While speaking in this manner, with his scourge
    A demon smote him, and said: "Get thee gone   65
    Pander, there are no women here for coin."

I joined myself again unto mine Escort;
    Thereafterward with footsteps few we came
    To where a crag projected from the bank.

This very easily did we ascend,   70
    And turning to the right along its ridge,
    From those eternal circles we departed.

When we were there, where it is hollowed out
    Beneath, to give a passage to the scourged,
    The Guide said: "Wait, and see that on thee strike   75

The vision of those others evil-born,
    Of whom thou hast not yet beheld the faces,
    Because together with us they have gone."

From the old bridge we looked upon the train
    Which tow'rds us came upon the other border,   80
    And which the scourges in like manner smite.

And the good Master, without my inquiring,
    Said to me: "See that tall one who is coming,
    And for his pain seems not to shed a tear;

Still what a royal aspect he retains!   85
    That Jason is, who by his heart and cunning
    The Colchians of the Ram made destitute.

He by the isle of Lemnos passed along
    After the daring women pitiless
    Had unto death devoted all their males.   90

There with his tokens and with ornate words
    Did he deceive Hypsipyle, the maiden
    Who first, herself, had all the rest deceived.

There did he leave her pregnant and forlorn;
    Such sin unto such punishment condemns him,   95
    And also for Medea[5] is vengeance done.

With him go those who in such wise deceive;
    And this sufficient be of the first valley
    To know, and those that in its jaws it holds."

We were already where the narrow path   100
    Crosses athwart the second dike, and forms
    Of that a buttress for another arch.

Thence we heard people, who are making moan
    In the next Bolgia, snorting with their muzzles,
    And with their palms beating upon themselves   105

The margins were encrusted with a mold
    By exhalation from below, that sticks there,
    And with the eyes and nostrils wages war.

The bottom is so deep, no place suffices
    To give us sight of it, without ascending   110
    The arch's back, where most the crag impends.

Thither we came, and thence down in the moat
    I saw a people smothered in a filth
    That out of human privies seemed to flow;

And whilst below there with mine eye I search,   115
    I saw one with his head so foul with ordure,
    It was not clear if he were clerk or layman.[6]

He screamed to me: "Wherefore art thou so eager
    To look at me more than the other foul ones?"
    And I to him: "Because, if I remember,   120

I have already seen thee with dry hair,
    And thou'rt Alessio Interminei[7] of Lucca;
    Therefore I eye thee more than all the others."

And he thereon, belaboring his pumpkin:
    "The flatteries have submerged me here below,   125
    Wherewith my tongue was never surfeited."

Then said to me the Guide: "See that thou thrust
    Thy visage somewhat farther in advance,
    That with thine eyes thou well the face attain

Of that uncleanly and disheveled drab,   130
    Who there doth scratch herself with filthy nails,
    And crouches now, and now on foot is standing.

Thais[8] the harlot is it, who replied
    Unto her paramour, when he said, 'Have I
    Great gratitude from thee?'—'Nay, marvelous';   135

And herewith let our sight be satisfied."

⤙ CANTO XIX ⤚

The Third Bolgia: Simoniacs—Pope Nicholas III—
Dante's Reproof of Corrupt Prelates

O Simon Magus,[1] O forlorn disciples,
Ye who the things of God, which ought to be
The brides of holiness, rapaciously

For silver and for gold do prostitute,
  Now it behoves for you the trumpet sound,   5
  Because in this third Bolgia ye abide.

We had already on the following tomb
  Ascended to that portion of the crag
  Which o'er the middle of the moat hangs plumb.

Wisdom supreme, O how great art thou showest   10
  In heaven, in earth, and in the evil world,
  And with what justice doth thy power distribute!

I saw upon the sides and on the bottom
  The livid stone with perforations filled,
  All of one size, and every one was round.   15

To me less ample seemed they not, nor greater
  Than those that in my beautiful Saint John
  Are fashioned for the place of the baptizers,

And one of which, not many years ago,
    I broke for some one, who was drowning in it;   20
    Be this a seal all men to undeceive.

Out of the mouth of each one there protruded
    The feet of a transgressor, and the legs
    Up to the calf, the rest within remained.

In all of them the soles were both on fire;   25
    Wherefore the joints so violently quivered,
    They would have snapped asunder withes and bands.

Even as the flame of unctuous things is wont
    To move upon the outer surface only,
    So likewise was it there from heel to point.   30

"Master, who is that one who writhes himself,
    More than his other comrades quivering,"
    I said, "and whom a redder flame is sucking?"

And he to me: "If thou wilt have me bear thee
    Down there along that bank which lowest lies,   35
    From him thou'lt know his errors and himself."

And I: "What pleases thee, to me is pleasing;
    Thou art my Lord, and knowest that I depart not
    From thy desire, and knowest what is not spoken."

Straightway upon the fourth dike we arrived;   40
    We turned, and on the left-hand side descended
    Down to the bottom full of holes and narrow.

And the good Master yet from off his haunch
    Deposed me not, till to the hole he brought me
    Of him who so lamented with his shanks.   45

"Whoe'er thou art, that standest upside down,
  O doleful soul, implanted like a stake,"
  To say began I, "if thou canst, speak out."

I stood even as the friar who is confessing
  The false assassin, who, when he is fixed,   50
  Recalls him, so that death may be delayed.

And he cried out: "Dost thou stand there already,
  Dost thou stand there already, Boniface?²
  By many years the record lied to me.

Art thou so early satiate with that wealth,   55
  For which thou didst not fear to take by fraud
  The beautiful Lady,³ and then work her woe?"

Such I became, as people are who stand,
  Not comprehending what is answered them,
  As if bemocked, and know not how to answer.   60

Then said Virgilius: "Say to him straightway,
  'I am not he, I am not he thou thinkest.'"
  And I replied as was imposed on me.

Whereat the spirit writhed with both his feet,
  Then, sighing, with a voice of lamentation   65
  Said to me: "Then what wantest thou of me?

If who I am thou carest so much to know,
  That thou on that account hast crossed the bank,
  Know that I vested was with the great mantle;

And truly was I son of the She-bear,⁴   70
  So eager to advance the cubs, that wealth
  Above, and here myself, I pocketed.

Beneath my head the others are dragged down
   Who have preceded me in simony,
   Flattened along the fissure of the rock.   75

Below there I shall likewise fall, whenever
   That one shall come who I believed thou wast,
   What time the sudden question I proposed.

But longer I my feet already toast,
   And here have been in this way upside down,   80
   Than he will planted stay with reddened feet;

For after him shall come of fouler deed
   From tow'rds the west a Pastor without law,[5]
   Such as befits to cover him and me.

New Jason will he be, of whom we read   85
   In Maccabees;[6] and as his king was pliant,
   So he who governs France shall be to this one."

I do not know if I were here too bold,
   That him I answered only in this meter:
   "I pray thee tell me now how great a treasure   90

Our Lord demanded of Saint Peter first,
   Before he put the keys into his keeping?
   Truly he nothing asked but 'Follow me.'

Nor Peter nor the rest asked of Matthias
   Silver or gold, when he by lot was chosen   95
   Unto the place the guilty soul had lost.

Therefore stay here, for thou art justly punished,
   And keep safe guard o'er the ill-gotten money,
   Which caused thee to be valiant against Charles.

And were it not that still forbids it me   100
    The reverence for the keys superlative
    Thou hadst in keeping in the gladsome life,

I would make use of words more grievous still;
    Because your avarice afflicts the world,
    Trampling the good and lifting the depraved.   105

The Evangelist you Pastors had in mind,
    When she who sitteth upon many waters
    To fornicate with kings by him was seen;

The same who with the seven heads was born,
    And power and strength from the ten horns[7] received, 110
    So long as virtue to her spouse was pleasing.

Ye have made yourselves a god of gold and silver;
    And from the idolater how differ ye,
    Save that he one, and ye a hundred worship?

Ah, Constantine![8] of how much ill was mother,   115
    Not thy conversion, but that marriage dower
    Which the first wealthy Father took from thee!"

And while I sang to him such notes as these,
    Either that anger or that conscience stung him,
    He struggled violently with both his feet.   120

I think in sooth that it my Leader pleased,
    With such contented lip he listened ever
    Unto the sound of the true words expressed.

Therefore with both his arms he took me up,
    And when he had me all upon his breast,   125
    Remounted by the way where he descended.

Nor did he tire to have me clasped to him;
  But bore me to the summit of the arch
  Which from the fourth dike to the fifth is passage.

There tenderly he laid his burden down,   130
  Tenderly on the crag uneven and steep,
  That would have been hard passage for the goats:

Thence was unveiled to me another valley.

⇥ CANTO XX ⇤

*The Fourth Bolgia: Soothsayers—Amphiaraus, Tiresias, Aruns,
Manto, Eryphylus, Michael Scott, Guido Bonatti, and Asdente—
Virgil Reproaches Dante's Pity—Mantua's Foundation*

OF A NEW PAIN BEHOVES ME TO MAKE VERSES
And give material to the twentieth canto
Of the first song, which is of the submerged.

I was already thoroughly disposed
    To peer down into the uncovered depth,
    Which bathed itself with tears of agony;   5

And people saw I through the circular valley,
    Silent and weeping, coming at the pace
    Which in this world the Litanies assume.

As lower down my sight descended on them,   10
    Wondrously each one seemed to be distorted
    From chin to the beginning of the chest;

For tow'rds the reins the countenance was turned,
    And backward it behoved them to advance,
    As to look forward had been taken from them.   15

Perchance indeed by violence of palsy
    Some one has been thus wholly turned awry;
    But I ne'er saw it, nor believe it can be.

As God may let thee, Reader, gather fruit
    From this thy reading, think now for thyself   20
    How I could ever keep my face unmoistened,

When our own image near me I beheld
    Distorted so, the weeping of the eyes
    Along the fissure bathed the hinder parts.

Truly I wept, leaning upon a peak   25
    Of the hard crag, so that my Escort said
    To me: "Art thou, too, of the other fools?

Here pity lives when it is wholly dead;
    Who is a greater reprobate than he
    Who feels compassion at the doom divine?   30

Lift up, lift up thy head, and see for whom
    Opened the earth before the Thebans' eyes;
    Wherefore they all cried: 'Whither rushest thou,

Amphiaraus?[1] Why dost leave the war?'
    And downward ceased he not to fall amain   35
    As far as Minos, who lays hold on all.

See, he has made a bosom of his shoulders!
    Because he wished to see too far before him
    Behind he looks, and backward goes his way:

Behold Tiresias, who his semblance changed,   40
    When from a male a female he became,
    His members being all of them transformed;

And afterwards was forced to strike once more
 The two entangled serpents[2] with his rod,
 Ere he could have again his manly plumes.   45

That Aruns is, who backs the other's belly,
 Who in the hills of Luni, there where grubs
 The Carrarese[3] who houses underneath,

Among the marbles white a cavern had
 For his abode; whence to behold the stars   50
 And sea, the view was not cut off from him.

And she there, who is covering up her breasts,
 Which thou beholdest not, with loosened tresses,
 And on that side has all the hairy skin,

Was Manto,[4] who made quest through many lands, 55
 Afterwards tarried there where I was born;
 Whereof I would thou list to me a little.

After her father had from life departed,
 And the city of Bacchus had become enslaved,
 She a long season wandered through the world. 60

Above in beauteous Italy lies a lake
 At the Alp's foot that shuts in Germany
 Over Tyrol, and has the name Benaco.

By a thousand springs, I think, and more, is bathed,
 'Twixt Garda and Val Camonica, Pennino,   65
 With water that grows stagnant in that lake.

Midway a place is where the Trentine Pastor,
 And he of Brescia, and the Veronese
 Might give his blessing, if he passed that way.

Sitteth Peschiera, fortress fair and strong,   70
   To front the Brescians and the Bergamasks,
   Where round about the bank descendeth lowest.

There of necessity must fall whatever
   In bosom of Benaco cannot stay,
   And grows a river down through verdant pastures.   75

Soon as the water doth begin to run,
   No more Benaco is it called, but Mincio,
   Far as Governo, where it falls in Po.

Not far it runs before it finds a plain
   In which it spreads itself, and makes it marshy,   80
   And oft 'tis wont in summer to be sickly.

Passing that way the virgin pitiless
   Land in the middle of the fen descried,
   Untilled and naked of inhabitants;

There to escape all human intercourse,   85
   She with her servants stayed, her arts to practice
   And lived, and left her empty body there.

The men, thereafter, who were scattered round,
   Collected in that place, which was made strong
   By the lagoon it had on every side;   90

They built their city over those dead bones,
   And, after her who first the place selected,
   Mantua named it, without other omen.

Its people once within more crowded were,
   Ere the stupidity of Casalodi   95
   From Pinamonte had received deceit.

Therefore I caution thee, if e'er thou hearest
    Originate my city otherwise,
    No falsehood may the verity defraud."

And I: "My Master, thy discourses are   100
    To me so certain, and so take my faith,
    That unto me the rest would be spent coals.

But tell me of the people who are passing,
    If any one noteworthy thou beholdest,
    For only unto that my mind reverts."   105

Then said he to me: "He who from the cheek
    Thrusts out his beard upon his swarthy shoulders
    Was, at the time when Greece was void of males,

So that there scarce remained one in the cradle,
    An augur, and with Calchas gave the moment,   110
    In Aulis, when to sever the first cable.

Eryphylus[5] his name was, and so sings
    My lofty Tragedy in some part or other;
    That knowest thou well, who knowest the whole of it.

The next, who is so slender in the flanks,   115
    Was Michael Scott,[6] who of a verity
    Of magical illusions knew the game.

Behold Guido Bonatti, behold Asdente,[7]
    Who now unto his leather and his thread
    Would fain have stuck, but he too late repents.   120

Behold the wretched ones, who left the needle,
    The spool and rock, and made them fortune-tellers;
    They wrought their magic spells with herb and image.

But come now, for already holds the confines
    Of both the hemispheres, and under Seville   125
    Touches the ocean-wave, Cain and the thorns,

And yesternight the moon was round already;
    Thou shouldst remember well it did not harm thee
    From time to time within the forest deep."

Thus spake he to me, and we walked the while.   130

⇥ CANTO XXI ⇤

The Fifth Bolgia: Peculators—The Elder of Santa Zita—
Malacoda and other Devils

FROM BRIDGE TO BRIDGE THUS, SPEAKING OTHER THINGS
Of which my Comedy cares not to sing,
We came along, and held the summit, when

We halted to behold another fissure
    Of Malebolge and other vain laments;   5
    And I beheld it marvelously dark.

As in the Arsenal¹ of the Venetians
    Boils in the winter the tenacious pitch
    To smear their unsound vessels o'er again,

For sail they cannot; and instead thereof   10
    One makes his vessel new, and one recaulks
    The ribs of that which many a voyage has made;

One hammers at the prow, one at the stern,
    This one makes oars, and that one cordage twists,
    Another mends the mainsail and the mizzen;   15

Thus, not by fire, but by the art divine,
    Was boiling down below there a dense pitch
    Which upon every side the bank belimed.

I saw it, but I did not see within it
    Aught but the bubbles that the boiling raised,   20
    And all swell up and resubside compressed.

The while below there fixedly I gazed,
    My Leader, crying out: "Beware, beware!"
    Drew me unto himself from where I stood.

Then I turned round, as one who is impatient   25
    To see what it behoves him to escape,
    And whom a sudden terror doth unman,

Who, while he looks, delays not his departure;
    And I beheld behind us a black devil,
    Running along upon the crag, approach.   30

Ah, how ferocious was he in his aspect!
    And how he seemed to me in action ruthless,
    With open wings and light upon his feet!

His shoulders, which sharp-pointed were and high,
    A sinner did encumber with both haunches,   35
    And he held clutched the sinews of the feet.

From off our bridge, he said: "O Malebranche,[2]
    Behold one of the elders of Saint Zita;
    Plunge him beneath, for I return for others

Unto that town, which is well furnished with them.   40
    All there are barrators,[3] except Bonturo;[4]
    No into Yes for money there is changed."

He hurled him down, and over the hard crag
    Turned round, and never was a mastiff loosened
    In so much hurry to pursue a thief.   45

The other sank, and rose again face downward;
    But the demons, under cover of the bridge,
    Cried: "Here the Santo Volto[5] has no place!

Here swims one otherwise than in the Serchio;[6]
    Therefore, if for our gaffs thou wishest not,   50
    Do not uplift thyself above the pitch."

They seized him then with more than a hundred rakes;
    They said: "It here behoves thee to dance covered,
    That, if thou canst, thou secretly mayest pilfer."

Not otherwise the cooks their scullions make   55
    Immerse into the middle of the caldron
    The meat with hooks, so that it may not float.

Said the good Master to me: "That it be not
    Apparent thou art here, crouch thyself down
    Behind a jag, that thou mayest have some screen;   60

And for no outrage that is done to me
    Be thou afraid, because these things I know,
    For once before was I in such a scuffle."

Then he passed on beyond the bridge's head,
    And as upon the sixth bank he arrived,   65
    Need was for him to have a steadfast front.

With the same fury, and the same uproar,
    As dogs leap out upon a mendicant,
    Who on a sudden begs, where'er he stops,

They issued from beneath the little bridge,   70
    And turned against him all their grappling-irons;
    But he cried out: "Be none of you malignant!

Before those hooks of yours lay hold of me,
    Let one of you step forward, who may hear me,
    And then take counsel as to grappling me."   75

They all cried out: "Let Malacoda[7] go";
    Whereat one started, and the rest stood still,
    And he came to him, saying: "What avails it?"

"Thinkest thou, Malacoda, to behold me
    Advanced into this place," my Master said,   80
    "Safe hitherto from all your skill of fence,

Without the will divine, and fate auspicious?
    Let me go on, for it in Heaven is willed
    That I another show this savage road."

Then was his arrogance so humbled in him,   85
    That he let fall his grapnel at his feet,
    And to the others said: "Now strike him not."

And unto me my Guide: "O thou, who sittest
    Among the splinters of the bridge crouched down,
    Securely now return to me again."   90

Wherefore I started and came swiftly to him;
    And all the devils forward thrust themselves,
    So that I feared they would not keep their compact.

And thus beheld I once afraid the soldiers
    Who issued under safeguard from Caprona,   95
    Seeing themselves among so many foes.

Close did I press myself with all my person
    Beside my Leader, and turned not mine eyes
    From off their countenance, which was not good.

They lowered their rakes, and "Wilt thou have me hit him,"   100
    They said to one another, "on the rump?"
    And answered: "Yes; see that thou nick him with it."

But the same demon who was holding parley
    With my Conductor turned him very quickly,
    And said: "Be quiet, be quiet, Scarmiglione";   105

Then said to us: "You can no farther go
    Forward upon this crag, because is lying
    All shattered, at the bottom, the sixth arch.

And if it still doth please you to go onward,
    Pursue your way along upon this rock;   110
    Near is another crag that yields a path.

Yesterday, five hours later than this hour,
    One thousand and two hundred sixty-six
    Years were complete, that here the way was broken.

I send in that direction some of mine   115
    To see if any one doth air himself;
    Go ye with them; for they will not be vicious.

Step forward, Alichino and Calcabrina,"
    Began he to cry out, "and thou, Cagnazzo;
    And Barbariccia, do thou guide the ten.   120

Come forward, Libicocco and Draghignazzo,
    And tuskèd Ciriatto and Graffiacane,
    And Farfarello and mad Rubicante;[8]

Search ye all round about the boiling pitch;
    Let these be safe as far as the next crag,   125
    That all unbroken passes o'er the dens."

"O me! what is it, Master, that I see?
  Pray let us go," I said, "without an escort,
  If thou knowest how, since for myself I ask none.

If thou art as observant as thy wont is,   130
  Dost thou not see that they do gnash their teeth,
  And with their brows are threatening woe to us?"

And he to me: "I will not have thee fear;
  Let them gnash on, according to their fancy,
  Because they do it for those boiling wretches."   135

Along the left-hand dike they wheeled about;
  But first had each one thrust his tongue between
  His teeth towards their leader for a signal;

And he had made a trumpet of his rump.

⊰ CANTO XXII ⊱

Ciampolo, Friar Gomita, and Michael Zanche—
The Malebranche Quarrel

I HAVE EREWHILE SEEN HORSEMEN MOVING CAMP,
Begin the storming, and their muster make,
And sometimes starting off for their escape;

Vaunt-couriers[1] have I seen upon your land,
   O Aretines,[2] and foragers go forth,   5
      Tournaments stricken, and the joustings run,

Sometimes with trumpets and sometimes with bells,
   With kettle-drums, and signals of the castles,
      And with our own, and with outlandish things,

But never yet with bagpipe so uncouth   10
   Did I see horsemen move, nor infantry,
      Nor ship by any sign of land or star.

We went upon our way with the ten demons;
   Ah, savage company! but in the church
      With saints, and in the tavern with the gluttons!   15

Ever upon the pitch was my intent,
   To see the whole condition of that Bolgia,
      And of the people who therein were burned.

Even as the dolphins, when they make a sign
    To mariners by arching of the back,   20
    That they should counsel take to save their vessel,

Thus sometimes, to alleviate his pain,
    One of the sinners would display his back,
    And in less time conceal it than it lightens.

As on the brink of water in a ditch   25
    The frogs stand only with their muzzles out,
    So that they hide their feet and other bulk,

So upon every side the sinners stood;
    But ever as Barbariccia near them came,
    Thus underneath the boiling they withdrew.   30

I saw, and still my heart doth shudder at it,
    One waiting thus, even as it comes to pass
    One frog remains, and down another dives;

And Graffiacan, who most confronted him,
    Grappled him by his tresses smeared with pitch,   35
    And drew him up, so that he seemed an otter.

I knew, before, the names of all of them,
    So had I noted them when they were chosen,
    And when they called each other, listened how.

"O Rubicante, see that thou do lay   40
    Thy claws upon him, so that thou mayst flay him,"
    Cried all together the accursed ones.

And I: "My Master, see to it, if thou canst,
    That thou mayst know who is the luckless wight,
    Thus come into his adversaries' hands."   45

Near to the side of him my Leader drew,
    Asked of him whence he was; and he replied:
    "I in the kingdom of Navarre was born;[3]

My mother placed me servant to a lord,
    For she had borne me to a ribald knave,   50
    Destroyer of himself and of his things.

Then I domestic was of good King Thibault;
    I set me there to practice barratry,
    For which I pay the reckoning in this heat."

And Ciriatto, from whose mouth projected,   55
    On either side, a tusk, as in a boar,
    Caused him to feel how one of them could rip.

Among malicious cats the mouse had come;
    But Barbariccia clasped him in his arms,
    And said: "Stand ye aside, while I enfork him."   60

And to my Master he turned round his head;
    "Ask him again," he said, "if more thou wish
    To know from him, before some one destroy him."

The Guide: "Now tell then of the other culprits;
    Knowest thou any one who is a Latian,   65
    Under the pitch?" And he: "I separated

Lately from one who was a neighbor to it;
    Would that I still were covered up with him,
    For I should fear not either claw nor hook!"

And Libicocco: "We have borne too much";   70
    And with his grapnel seized him by the arm,
    So that, by rending, he tore off a tendon.

Eke Draghignazzo wished to pounce upon him
    Down at the legs; whence their Decurion
    Turned round and round about with evil look.   75

When they again somewhat were pacified,
    Of him, who still was looking at his wound,
    Demanded my Conductor without stay:

"Who was that one, from whom a luckless parting
    Thou sayest thou hast made, to come ashore?"   80
    And he replied: "It was the Friar Gomita,[4]

He of Gallura, vessel of all fraud,
    Who had the enemies of his Lord in hand,
    And dealt so with them each exults thereat;

Money he took, and let them smoothly off,   85
    As he says; and in other offices
    A barrator was he, not mean but sovereign.

Foregathers with him one Don Michel Zanche[5]
    Of Logodoro; and of Sardinia
    To gossip never do their tongues feel tired.   90

O me! see that one, how he grinds his teeth;
    Still farther would I speak, but am afraid
    Lest he to scratch my itch be making ready."

And the grand Provost, turned to Farfarello,
    Who rolled his eyes about as if to strike,   95
    Said: "Stand aside there, thou malicious bird."

"If you desire either to see or hear,"
    The terror-stricken recommenced thereon,
    "Tuscans or Lombards, I will make them come.

But let the Malebranche cease a little,   100
    So that these may not their revenges fear,
    And I, down sitting in this very place,

For one that I am will make seven come,
    When I shall whistle, as our custom is
    To do whenever one of us comes out."   105

Cagnazzo at these words his muzzle lifted,
    Shaking his head, and said: "Just hear the trick
    Which he has thought of, down to throw himself!"

Whence he, who snares in great abundance had,
    Responded: "I by far too cunning am,   110
    When I procure for mine a greater sadness."

Alichin held not in, but running counter
    Unto the rest, said to him: "If thou dive,
    I will not follow thee upon the gallop,

But I will beat my wings above the pitch;   115
    The height be left, and be the bank a shield
    To see if thou alone dost countervail us."

O thou who readest, thou shalt hear new sport!
    Each to the other side his eyes averted;
    He first, who most reluctant was to do it.   120

The Navarrese selected well his time;
    Planted his feet on land, and in a moment
    Leaped, and released himself from their design.

Whereat each one was suddenly stung with shame,
    But he most who was cause of the defeat;   125
    Therefore he moved, and cried: "Thou art o'ertaken."

But little it availed, for wings could not
    Outstrip the fear; the other one went under,
    And, flying, upward he his breast directed;

Not otherwise the duck upon a sudden   130
    Dives under, when the falcon is approaching,
    And upward he returneth cross and weary.

Infuriate at the mockery, Calcabrina
    Flying behind him followed close, desirous
    The other should escape, to have a quarrel.   135

And when the barrator had disappeared,
    He turned his talons upon his companion,
    And grappled with him right above the moat.

But sooth the other was a doughty sparhawk
    To clapperclaw him well; and both of them   140
    Fell in the middle of the boiling pond.

A sudden intercessor was the heat;
    But ne'ertheless of rising there was naught,
    To such degree they had their wings belimed.

Lamenting with the others, Barbariccia   145
    Made four of them fly to the other side
    With all their gaffs, and very speedily

This side and that they to their posts descended;
    They stretched their hooks towards the pitch-ensnared,
    Who were already baked within the crust,   150

And in this manner busied did we leave them.

⊰ CANTO XXIII ⊱

Escape from the Malebranche—The Sixth Bolgia: Hypocrites—
Catalano and Loderingo—Caiaphas

Silent, alone, and without company
We went, the one in front, the other after,
As go the Minor Friars[1] along their way.

Upon the fable of Æsop was directed
   My thought, by reason of the present quarrel,   5
   Where he has spoken of the frog and mouse;[2]

For *mo* and *issa*[3] are not more alike
   Than this one is to that, if well we couple
   End and beginning with a steadfast mind.

And even as one thought from another springs,   10
   So afterward from that was born another,
   Which the first fear within me double made.

Thus did I ponder: "These on our account
   Are laughed to scorn, with injury and scoff
   So great, that much I think it must annoy them.   15

If anger be engrafted on ill will,
   They will come after us more merciless
   Than dog upon the leveret which he seizes,"

I felt my hair stand all on end already
    With terror, and stood backwardly intent,   20
    When said I: "Master, if thou hidest not

Thyself and me forthwith, of Malebranche
    I am in dread; we have them now behind us;
    I so imagine them, I already feel them."

And he: "If I were made of leaded glass,   25
    Thine outward image I should not attract
    Sooner to me than I imprint the inner.

Just now thy thoughts came in among my own,
    With similar attitude and similar face,
    So that of both one counsel sole I made.   30

If peradventure the right bank so slope
    That we to the next Bolgia can descend,
    We shall escape from the imagined chase."

Not yet he finished rendering such opinion,
    When I beheld them come with outstretched wings,   35
    Not far remote, with will to seize upon us.

My Leader on a sudden seized me up,
    Even as a mother who by noise is wakened,
    And close beside her sees the enkindled flames,

Who takes her son, and flies, and does not stop,   40
    Having more care of him than of herself,
    So that she clothes her only with a shift;

And downward from the top of the hard bank
    Supine he gave him to the pendent rock,
    That one side of the other Bolgia walls.   45

Ne'er ran so swiftly water through a sluice
    To turn the wheel of any land-built mill,
    When nearest to the paddles it approaches,

As did my Master down along that border,
    Bearing me with him on his breast away,   50
    As his own son, and not as a companion.

Hardly the bed of the ravine below
    His feet had reached, ere they had reached the hill
    Right over us; but he was not afraid;

For the high Providence, which had ordained   55
    To place them ministers of the fifth moat,
    The power of thence departing took from all.

A painted people there below we found,
    Who went about with footsteps very slow,
    Weeping and in their semblance tired and vanquished. 60

They had on mantles with the hoods low down
    Before their eyes, and fashioned of the cut
    That in Cologne[4] they for the monks are made.

Without, they gilded are so that it dazzles;
    But inwardly all leaden and so heavy   65
    That Frederick[5] used to put them on of straw.

O everlastingly fatiguing mantle!
    Again we turned us, still to the left hand
    Along with them, intent on their sad plaint;

But owing to the weight, that weary folk   70
    Came on so tardily, that we were new
    In company at each motion of the haunch.

Whence I unto my Leader: "See thou find
    Some one who may by deed or name be known,
    And thus in going move thine eye about."   75

And one, who understood the Tuscan speech,
    Cried to us from behind: "Stay ye your feet,
    Ye, who so run athwart the dusky air!

Perhaps thou'lt have from me what thou demandest."
    Whereat the Leader turned him, and said: "Wait,   80
    And then according to his pace proceed."

I stopped, and two beheld I show great haste
    Of spirit, in their faces, to be with me;
    But the burden and the narrow way delayed them.

When they came up, long with an eye askance   85
    They scanned me without uttering a word.
    Then to each other turned, and said together:

"He by the action of his throat seems living;
    And if they dead are, by what privilege
    Go they uncovered by the heavy stole?"   90

Then said to me: "Tuscan, who to the college
    Of miserable hypocrites art come,
    Do not disdain to tell us who thou art."

And I to them: "Born was I, and grew up
    In the great town on the fair river of Arno,   95
    And with the body am I've always had.

But who are ye, in whom there trickles down
    Along your cheeks such grief as I behold?
    And what pain is upon you, that so sparkles?"

And one replied to me: "These orange cloaks   100
    Are made of lead so heavy, that the weights
    Cause in this way their balances to creak.

Frati Gaudenti were we, and Bolognese;
    I Catalano, and he Loderingo[6]
    Named, and together taken by thy city,   105

As the wont is to take one man alone,
    For maintenance of its peace; and we were such
    That still it is apparent round Gardingo."

"O Friars," began I, "your iniquitous . . ."
    But said no more; for to mine eyes there rushed   110
    One crucified with three stakes on the ground.

When me he saw, he writhed himself all over,
    Blowing into his beard with suspirations;
    And the Friar Catalan, who noticed this,

Said to me: "This transfixed one,[7] whom thou seest,   115
    Counselled the Pharisees that it was meet
    To put one man to torture for the people.

Crosswise and naked is he on the path,
    As thou perceivest; and he needs must feel,
    Whoever passes, first how much he weighs;   120

And in like mode his father-in-law is punished
    Within this moat, and the others of the council,
    Which for the Jews was a malignant seed."

And thereupon I saw Virgilius marvel
    O'er him who was extended on the cross   125
    So vilely in eternal banishment.

Then he directed to the Friar this voice:
    "Be not displeased, if granted thee, to tell us
    If to the right hand any pass slope down

By which we two may issue forth from here,   130
    Without constraining some of the black angels
    To come and extricate us from this deep."

Then he made answer: "Nearer than thou hopest
    There is a rock, that forth from the great circle
    Proceeds, and crosses all the cruel valleys,   135

Save that at this 'tis broken, and does not bridge it;
    You will be able to mount up the ruin,
    That sidelong slopes and at the bottom rises."

The Leader stood awhile with head bowed down;
    Then said: "The business badly he recounted   140
    Who grapples with his hook the sinners yonder."

And the Friar: "Many of the Devil's vices
    Once heard I at Bologna, and among them,
    That he's a liar and the father of lies."

Thereat my Leader with great strides went on,   145
    Somewhat disturbed with anger in his looks;
    Whence from the heavy-laden I departed

After the prints of his beloved feet.

⊰ CANTO XXIV ⊱

The Seventh Bolgia: Thieves—Vanni Fucci—Serpents

IN THAT PART OF THE YOUTHFUL YEAR WHEREIN
The Sun his locks beneath Aquarius tempers,
And now the nights draw near to half the day,

What time the hoar-frost copies on the ground
   The outward semblance of her sister white,   5
   But little lasts the temper of her pen,

The husbandman, whose forage faileth him,
   Rises, and looks, and seeth the champaign[1]
   All gleaming white, whereat he beats his flank,

Returns in doors, and up and down laments,   10
   Like a poor wretch, who knows not what to do;
   Then he returns and hope revives again,

Seeing the world has changed its countenance
   In little time, and takes his shepherd's crook,
   And forth the little lambs to pasture drives.   15

Thus did the Master fill me with alarm,
   When I beheld his forehead so disturbed,
   And to the ailment came as soon the plaster.

For as we came unto the ruined bridge,
    The Leader turned to me with that sweet look   20
    Which at the mountain's foot I first beheld.

His arms he opened, after some advisement
    Within himself elected, looking first
    Well at the ruin, and laid hold of me.

And even as he who acts and meditates,   25
    For aye it seems that he provides beforehand,
    So upward lifting me towards the summit

Of a huge rock, he scanned another crag,
    Saying: "To that one grapple afterwards,
    But try first if 'tis such that it will hold thee."   30

This was no way for one clothed with a cloak;
    For hardly we, he light, and I pushed upward,
    Were able to ascend from jag to jag.

And had it not been, that upon that precinct
    Shorter was the ascent than on the other,   35
    He I know not, but I had been dead beat.

But because Malebolge tow'rds the mouth
    Of the profoundest well is all inclining,
    The structure of each valley doth import

That one bank rises and the other sinks.   40
    Still we arrived at length upon the point
    Wherefrom the last stone breaks itself asunder.

The breath was from my lungs so milked away,
    When I was up, that I could go no farther,
    Nay, I sat down upon my first arrival.   45

"Now it behoves thee thus to put off sloth,"
    My Master said; "for sitting upon down,
    Or under quilt, one cometh not to fame,

Withouten which whoso his life consumes
    Such vestige leaveth of himself on earth,   50
    As smoke in air or in the water foam.

And therefore raise thee up, o'ercome the anguish
    With spirit that o'ercometh every battle,
    If with its heavy body it sink not.

A longer stairway it behoves thee mount;   55
    'Tis not enough from these to have departed;
    Let it avail thee, if thou understand me."

Then I uprose, showing myself provided
    Better with breath than I did feel myself,
    And said: "Go on, for I am strong and bold."   60

Upward we took our way along the crag,
    Which jagged was, and narrow, and difficult,
    And more precipitous far than that before.

Speaking I went, not to appear exhausted;
    Whereat a voice from the next moat came forth,   65
    Not well adapted to articulate words.

I know not what it said, though o'er the back
    I now was of the arch that passes there;
    But he seemed moved to anger who was speaking.

I was bent downward, but my living eyes   70
    Could not attain the bottom, for the dark;
    Wherefore I: "Master, see that thou arrive

At the next round, and let us descend the wall;
    For as from hence I hear and understand not,
    So I look down and nothing I distinguish."   75

"Other response," he said, "I make thee not,
    Except the doing; for the modest asking
    Ought to be followed by the deed in silence."

We from the bridge descended at its head,
    Where it connects itself with the eighth bank,   80
    And then was manifest to me the Bolgia;

And I beheld therein a terrible throng
    Of serpents, and of such a monstrous kind,
    That the remembrance still congeals my blood.

Let Libya boast no longer with her sand;   85
    For if Chelydri, Jaculi, and Pharæ
    She breeds, with Cenchri and with Amphisbæna,[2]

Neither so many plagues nor so malignant
    E'er showed she with all Ethiopia,
    Nor with whatever on the Red Sea is!   90

Among this cruel and most dismal throng
    People were running naked and affrighted.
    Without the hope of hole or heliotrope.

They had their hands with serpents bound behind them;
    These riveted upon their reins the tail   95
    And head, and were in front of them entwined.

And lo! at one who was upon our side
    There darted forth a serpent, which transfixed him
    There where the neck is knotted to the shoulders.

Nor *O* so quickly e'er, nor *I* was written,   100
 As he took fire, and burned; and ashes wholly
 Behoved it that in falling he became.

And when he on the ground was thus destroyed,
 The ashes drew together, and of themselves
 Into himself they instantly returned.   105

Even thus by the great sages 'tis confessed
 The phoenix dies, and then is born again,
 When it approaches its five-hundredth year;

On herb or grain it feeds not in its life,
 But only on tears of incense and amomum,   110
 And nard and myrrh are its last winding-sheet.

And as he is who falls, and knows not how,
 By force of demons who to earth down drag him,
 Or other oppilation³ that binds man,

When he arises and around him looks,   115
 Wholly bewildered by the mighty anguish
 Which he has suffered, and in looking sighs;

Such was that sinner after he had risen.
 Justice of God! O how severe it is,
 That blows like these in vengeance poureth down!   120

The Guide thereafter asked him who he was;
 Whence he replied: "I rained from Tuscany
 A short time since into this cruel gorge.

A bestial life, and not a human, pleased me,
 Even as the mule I was; I'm Vanni Fucci,⁴   125
 Beast, and Pistoia was my worthy den."

And I unto the Guide: "Tell him to stir not,
    And ask what crime has thrust him here below,
    For once a man of blood and wrath I saw him."

And the sinner, who had heard, dissembled not,   130
    But unto me directed mind and face,
    And with a melancholy shame was painted.

Then said: "It pains me more that thou hast caught me
    Amid this misery where thou seest me,
    Than when I from the other life was taken.   135

What thou demandest I cannot deny;
    So low am I put down because I robbed
    The sacristy of the fair ornaments,

And falsely once 'twas laid upon another;
    But that thou mayst not such a sight enjoy,   140
    If thou shalt e'er be out of the dark places,

Thine ears to my announcement ope and hear:
    Pistoia first of Neri groweth meager;
    Then Florence doth renew her men and manners;

Mars draws a vapor up from Val di Magra,   145
    Which is with turbid clouds enveloped round,
    And with impetuous and bitter tempest

Over Campo Picen shall be the battle;
    When it shall suddenly rend the mist asunder,
    So that each Bianco[5] shall thereby be smitten.   150

And this I've said that it may give thee pain."

⧏ CANTO XXV ⧐

Vanni Fucci's Punishment—Agnello Brunelleschi, Buoso degli Abati,
Puccio Sciancato, Cianfa de' Donati, and Guercio Cavalcanti

AT THE CONCLUSION OF HIS WORDS, THE THIEF
Lifted his hands aloft with both the figs,[1]
Crying: "Take that, God, for at thee I aim them."

From that time forth the serpents were my friends;
    For one entwined itself about his neck   5
    As if it said: "I will not thou speak more";

And round his arms another, and rebound him,
    Clinching itself together so in front,
    That with them he could not a motion make.

Pistoia, ah, Pistoia! why resolve not   10
    To burn thyself to ashes and so perish,
    Since in ill-doing thou thy seed excellest?

Through all the somber circles of this Hell,
    Spirit I saw not against God so proud,
    Not he who fell at Thebes down from the walls!   15

He fled away, and spake no further word;
    And I beheld a Centaur full of rage
Come crying out: "Where is, where is the scoffer?"

142

I do not think Maremma² has so many
    Serpents as he had all along his back,   20
    As far as where our countenance begins.

Upon the shoulders, just behind the nape,
    With wings wide open was a dragon lying,
    And he sets fire to all that he encounters.

My Master said: "That one is Cacus,³ who   25
    Beneath the rock upon Mount Aventine
    Created oftentimes a lake of blood.

He goes not on the same road with his brothers,
    By reason of the fraudulent theft he made
    Of the great herd, which he had near to him;   30

Whereat his tortuous actions ceased beneath
    The mace of Hercules,⁴ who peradventure
    Gave him a hundred, and he felt not ten."

While he was speaking thus, he had passed by,
    And spirits three had underneath us come,   35
    Of which nor I aware was, nor my Leader,

Until what time they shouted: "Who are you?"
    On which account our story made a halt,
    And then we were intent on them alone.

I did not know them; but it came to pass,   40
    As it is wont to happen by some chance,
    That one to name the other was compelled,

Exclaiming: "Where can Cianfa⁵ have remained?"
    Whence I, so that the Leader might attend,
    Upward from chin to nose my finger laid.   45

If thou art, Reader, slow now to believe
    What I shall say, it will no marvel be,
    For I who saw it hardly can admit it.

As I was holding raised on them my brows,
    Behold! a serpent with six feet darts forth   50
    In front of one, and fastens wholly on him.

With middle feet it bound him round the paunch,
    And with the forward ones his arms it seized;
    Then thrust its teeth through one cheek and the other;

The hindermost it stretched upon his thighs,   55
    And put its tail through in between the two,
    And up behind along the reins outspread it.

Ivy was never fastened by its barbs
    Unto a tree so, as this horrible reptile
    Upon the other's limbs entwined its own.   60

Then they stuck close, as if of heated wax
    They had been made, and intermixed their color;
    Nor one nor other seemed now what he was;

E'en as proceedeth on before the flame
    Upward along the paper a brown color,   65
    Which is not black as yet, and the white dies.

The other two looked on, and each of them
    Cried out: "O me, Agnello,[6] how thou changest!
    Behold, thou now art neither two nor one."

Already the two heads had one become,   70
    When there appeared to us two figures mingled
    Into one face, wherein the two were lost.

Of the four lists were fashioned the two arms,
    The thighs and legs, the belly and the chest
    Members became that never yet were seen.   75

Every original aspect there was canceled;
    Two and yet none did the perverted image
    Appear, and such departed with slow pace.

Even as a lizard, under the great scourge
    Of days canicular,[7] exchanging hedge,   80
    Lightning appeareth if the road it cross;

Thus did appear, coming towards the bellies
    Of the two others, a small fiery serpent,
    Livid and black as is a peppercorn.

And in that part whereat is first received   85
    Our aliment,[8] it one of them transfixed;
    Then downward fell in front of him extended.

The one transfixed looked at it, but said naught;
    Nay, rather with feet motionless he yawned,
    Just as if sleep or fever had assailed him.   90

He at the serpent gazed, and it at him;
    One through the wound, the other through the mouth
    Smoked violently, and the smoke commingled.

Henceforth be silent Lucan, where he mentions
    Wretched Sabellus and Nassidius,[9]   95
    And wait to hear what now shall be shot forth.

Be silent Ovid, of Cadmus and Arethusa;[10]
    For if him to a snake, her to fountain,
    Converts he fabling, that I grudge him not;

Because two natures never front to front   100
    Has he transmuted, so that both the forms
    To interchange their matter ready were.

Together they responded in such wise,
    That to a fork the serpent cleft his tail,
    And eke the wounded drew his feet together.   105

The legs together with the thighs themselves
    Adhered so, that in little time the juncture
    No sign whatever made that was apparent.

He with the cloven tail assumed the figure
    The other one was losing, and his skin   110
    Became elastic, and the other's hard.

I saw the arms draw inward at the armpits,
    And both feet of the reptile, that were short,
    Lengthen as much as those contracted were.

Thereafter the hind feet, together twisted,   115
    Became the member that a man conceals,
    And of his own the wretch had two created.

While both of them the exhalation veils
    With a new color, and engenders hair
    On one of them and depilates the other,   120

The one uprose and down the other fell,
    Though turning not away their impious lamps,
    Underneath which each one his muzzle changed.

He who was standing drew it tow'rds the temples,
    And from excess of matter, which came thither,   125
    Issued the ears from out the hollow cheeks;

What did not backward run and was retained
    Of that excess made to the face a nose,
    And the lips thickened far as was befitting.

He who lay prostrate thrusts his muzzle forward,   130
    And backward draws the ears into his head,
    In the same manner as the snail its horns;

And so the tongue, which was entire and apt
    For speech before, is cleft, and the bi-forked
    In the other closes up, and the smoke ceases.   135

The soul, which to a reptile had been changed,
    Along the valley hissing takes to flight,
    And after him the other speaking sputters.

Then did he turn upon him his new shoulders,
    And said to the other: "I'll have Buoso[11] run,   140
    Crawling as I have done, along this road."

In this way I beheld the seventh ballast
    Shift and reshift, and here be my excuse
    The novelty, if aught my pen transgress.

And notwithstanding that mine eyes might be   145
    Somewhat bewildered, and my mind dismayed,
    They could not flee away so secretly

But that I plainly saw Puccio Sciancato;[12]
    And he it was who sole of three companions,
    Which came in the beginning, was not changed;   150

The other was he whom thou, Gaville,[13] weepest.

⊰ CANTO XXVI ⊱

The Eighth Bolgia: Evil Counselors—Ulysses and Diomed—
Ulysses' Last Voyage

REJOICE, O FLORENCE, SINCE THOU ART SO GREAT,
That over sea and land thou beatest thy wings,
And throughout Hell thy name is spread abroad!

Among the thieves five citizens of thine
    Like these I found, whence shame comes unto me,   5
    And thou thereby to no great honor risest.

But if when morn is near our dreams are true,
    Feel shalt thou in a little time from now
    What Prato,¹ if none other, craves for thee.

And if it now were, it were not too soon;   10
    Would that it were, seeing it needs must be,
    For 'twill aggrieve me more the more I age.

We went our way, and up along the stairs
    The bourns² had made us to descend before,
    Remounted my Conductor and drew me.   15

And following the solitary path
    Among the rocks and ridges of the crag,
    The foot without the hand sped not at all.

Then sorrowed I, and sorrow now again,
    When I direct my mind to what I saw,   20
    And more my genius curb than I am wont,

That it may run not unless virtue guide it;
    So that if some good star, or better thing,
    Have given me good, I may myself not grudge it.

As many as the hind (who on the hill   25
    Rests at the time when he who lights the world
    His countenance keeps least concealed from us,

While as the fly gives place unto the gnat)
    Seeth the glow-worms down along the valley,
    Perchance there where he ploughs and makes his vintage; 30

With flames as manifold resplendent all
    Was the eighth Bolgia, as I grew aware
    As soon as I was where the depth appeared.

And such as he who with the bears avenged him
    Beheld Elijah's chariot³ at departing,   35
    What time the steeds to heaven erect uprose,

For with his eye he could not follow it
    So as to see aught else than flame alone,
    Even as a little cloud ascending upward,

Thus each along the gorge of the intrenchment   40
    Was moving; for not one reveals the theft,
    And every flame a sinner steals away.

I stood upon the bridge uprisen to see,
    So that, if I had seized not on a rock,
    Down had I fallen without being pushed.   45

And the Leader, who beheld me so attent,
　　Exclaimed: "Within the fires the spirits are;
　　Each swathes himself with that wherewith he burns."

"My Master," I replied, "by hearing thee
　　I am more sure; but I surmised already　　　　　　50
　　It might be so, and already wished to ask thee

Who is within that fire, which comes so cleft
　　At top, it seems uprising from the pyre
　　Where was Eteocles with his brother⁴ placed."

He answered me: "Within there are tormented　　　　55
　　Ulysses and Diomed, and thus together
　　They unto vengeance run as unto wrath.

And there within their flame do they lament
　　The ambush of the horse, which made the door
　　Whence issued forth the Romans' gentle seed;⁵　　60

Therein is wept the craft, for which being dead
　　Deidamia still deplores Achilles,
　　And pain for the Palladium⁶ there is borne."

"If they within those sparks possess the power
　　To speak," I said, "thee, Master, much I pray,　　65
　　And re-pray, that the prayer be worth a thousand,

That thou make no denial of awaiting
　　Until the hornëd flame shall hither come;
　　Thou seest that with desire I lean towards it."

And he to me: "Worthy is thy entreaty　　　　　　70
　　Of much applause, and therefore I accept it;
　　But take heed that thy tongue restrain itself.

Leave me to speak, because I have conceived
    That which thou wishest; for they might disdain
    Perchance, since they were Greeks, discourse of thine."   75

When now the flame had come unto that point,
    Where to my Leader it seemed time and place,
    After this fashion did I hear him speak:

"O ye, who are twofold within one fire,
    If I deserved of you, while I was living,   80
    If I deserved of you or much or little

When in the world I wrote the lofty verses,
    Do not move on, but one of you declare
    Whither, being lost, he went away to die."

Then of the antique flame the greater horn,   85
    Murmuring, began to wave itself about
    Even as a flame doth which the wind fatigues.

Thereafterward, the summit to and fro
    Moving as if it were the tongue that spake,
    It uttered forth a voice, and said: "When I   90

From Circe had departed, who concealed me
    More than a year there near unto Gaëta,
    Or ever yet Æneas[7] named it so,

Nor fondness for my son, nor reverence
    For my old father, nor the due affection   95
    Which joyous should have made Penelope,[8]

Could overcome within me the desire
    I had to be experienced of the world,
    And of the vice and virtue of mankind;

But I put forth on the high open sea   100
    With one sole ship, and that small company
    By which I never had deserted been.

Both of the shores I saw as far as Spain,
    Far as Morocco, and the isle of Sardes,[9]
    And the others which that sea bathes round about.   105

I and my company were old and slow
    When at that narrow passage we arrived
    Where Hercules his landmarks set as signals,[10]

That man no farther onward should adventure.
    On the right hand behind me left I Seville,   110
    And on the other already had left Ceuta.

'O brothers, who amid a hundred thousand
    Perils,' I said, 'have come unto the West,
    To this so inconsiderable vigil

Which is remaining of your senses still   115
    Be ye unwilling to deny the knowledge,
    Following the sun, of the unpeopled world.

Consider ye the seed from which ye sprang;
    Ye were not made to live like unto brutes,
    But for pursuit of virtue and of knowledge.'   120

So eager did I render my companions,
    With this brief exhortation, for the voyage,
    That then I hardly could have held them back.

And having turned our stern unto the morning,
    We of the oars made wings for our mad flight,   125
    Evermore gaining on the larboard side.

Already all the stars of the other pole
    The night beheld, and ours so very low
    It did not rise above the ocean floor.

Five times rekindled and as many quenched   130
    Had been the splendor underneath the moon,[11]
    Since we had entered into the deep pass,

When there appeared to us a mountain, dim
    From distance, and it seemed to me so high
    As I had never any one beheld.   135

Joyful were we, and soon it turned to weeping;
    For out of the new land a whirlwind rose,
    And smote upon the fore part of the ship.

Three times it made her whirl with all the waters,
    At the fourth time it made the stern uplift,   140
    And the prow downward go, as pleased Another,

Until the sea above us closed again."

⊰ CANTO XXVII ⊱

Guido da Montefeltro—His Deception by Pope Boniface VIII

ALREADY WAS THE FLAME ERECT AND QUIET,
To speak no more, and now departed from us
With the permission of the gentle Poet;

When yet another, which behind it came,
    Caused us to turn our eyes upon its top   5
    By a confused sound that issued from it.

As the Sicilian bull[1] (that bellowed first
    With the lament of him, and that was right,
    Who with his file had modulated it)

Bellowed so with the voice of the afflicted,   10
    That, notwithstanding it was made of brass,
    Still it appeared with agony transfixed;

Thus, by not having any way or issue
    At first from out the fire, to its own language
    Converted were the melancholy words.   15

But afterwards, when they had gathered way
    Up through the point, giving it that vibration
    The tongue had given them in their passage out,

We heard it said: "O thou, at whom I aim
    My voice,[2] and who but now wast speaking Lombard,   20
    Saying, 'Now go thy way, no more I urge thee,'

Because I come perchance a little late,
    To stay and speak with me let it not irk thee;
    Thou seest it irks not me, and I am burning.

If thou but lately into this blind world   25
    Hast fallen down from that sweet Latian land,
    Wherefrom I bring the whole of my transgression,

Say, if the Romagnuols[3] have peace or war,
    For I was from the mountains there between
    Urbino and the yoke whence Tiber bursts."   30

I still was downward bent and listening,
    When my Conductor touched me on the side,
    Saying: "Speak thou: this one a Latian is."

And I, who had beforehand my reply
    In readiness, forthwith began to speak: 35
    "O soul, that down below there art concealed,

Romagna thine is not and never has been
    Without war in the bosom of its tyrants;
    But open war I none have left there now.

Ravenna stands as it long years has stood;   40
    The Eagle of Polenta there is brooding,
    So that she covers Cervia[4] with her vans.

The city which once made the long resistance,
    And of the French a sanguinary heap,
    Beneath the Green Paws[5] finds itself again;   45

Verrucchio's ancient Mastiff and the new,
    Who made such bad disposal of Montagna,
    Where they are wont make wimbles[6] of their teeth.

The cities of Lamone and Santerno
    Governs the Lioncel of the white lair,[7]   50
    Who changes sides 'twixt summertime and winter;

And that of which the Savio[8] bathes the flank,
    Even as it lies between the plain and mountain,
    Lives between tyranny and a free state.

Now I entreat thee tell us who thou art;   55
    Be not more stubborn than the rest have been,
    So may thy name hold front there in the world."

After the fire a little more had roared
    In its own fashion, the sharp point it moved
    This way and that, and then gave forth such breath: 60

"If I believed that my reply were made
    To one who to the world would e'er return,
    This flame without more flickering would stand still;

But inasmuch as never from this depth
    Did any one return, if I hear true,   65
    Without the fear of infamy I answer,

I was a man of arms, then Cordelier,[9]
    Believing thus begirt to make amends;
    And truly my belief had been fulfilled

But for the High Priest,[10] whom may ill betide,   70
    Who put me back into my former sins;
    And how and wherefore I will have thee hear.

While I was still the form of bone and pulp
    My mother gave to me, the deeds I did
    Were not those of a lion, but a fox.   75

The machinations and the covert ways
    I knew them all, and practiced so their craft,
    That to the ends of earth the sound went forth.

When now unto that portion of mine age
    I saw myself arrived, when each one ought   80
    To lower the sails, and coil away the ropes,

That which before had pleased me then displeased me;
    And penitent and confessing I surrendered,
    Ah woe is me! and it would have bestead me;

The Leader of the modern Pharisees   85
    Having a war near unto Lateran,
    And not with Saracens nor with the Jews,

For each one of his enemies was Christian,
    And none of them had been to conquer Acre,
    Nor merchandising in the Sultan's land,   90

Nor the high office, nor the sacred orders,
    In him regarded, nor in me that cord
    Which used to make those girt with it more meager;

But even as Constantine sought out Sylvester
    To cure his leprosy, within Soracte,[11]   95
    So this one sought me out as an adept

To cure him of the fever of his pride.
    Counsel he asked of me, and I was silent,
    Because his words appeared inebriate.

And then he said: 'Be not thy heart afraid;   100
    Henceforth I thee absolve; and thou instruct me
    How to raze Palestrina[12] to the ground.

Heaven have I power to lock and to unlock,
    As thou dost know; therefore the keys are two,
    The which my predecessor held not dear.'   105

Then urged me on his weighty arguments
    There, where my silence was the worst advice;
    And said I: 'Father, since thou washest me

Of that sin into which I now must fall,
    The promise long with the fulfillment short   110
    Will make thee triumph in thy lofty seat.'

Francis came afterward, when I was dead,
    For me; but one of the black Cherubim[13]
    Said to him: 'Take him not; do me no wrong;

He must come down among my servitors,   115
    Because he gave the fraudulent advice
    From which time forth I have been at his hair;

For who repents not cannot be absolved,
    Nor can one both repent and will at once,
    Because of the contradiction which consents not.'   120

O miserable me! how I did shudder
    When he seized on me, saying: 'Peradventure
    Thou didst not think that I was a logician!'

He bore me unto Minos, who entwined
    Eight times his tail about his stubborn back,   125
    And after he had bitten it in great rage,

Said: 'Of the thievish fire a culprit this';
    Wherefore, here where thou seest, am I lost,
    And vested thus in going I bemoan me."

When it had thus completed its recital,   130
    The flame departed uttering lamentations,
    Writhing and flapping its sharp-pointed horn.

Onward we passed, both I and my Conductor,
    Up o'er the crag above another arch,
    Which the moat covers, where is paid the fee   135

By those who, sowing discord, win their burden.

⫷ CANTO XXVIII ⫸

The Ninth Bolgia: Schismatics—Mahomet and Ali—
Pier da Medicina, Curio, Mosca, and Bertrand de Born

WHO EVER COULD, E'EN WITH UNTRAMMELLED WORDS,
Tell of the blood and of the wounds in full
Which now I saw, by many times narrating?

Each tongue would for a certainty fall short
    By reason of our speech and memory,   5
    That have small room to comprehend so much.

If were again assembled all the people
    Which formerly upon the fateful land
    Of Puglia were lamenting for their blood

Shed by the Romans and the lingering war   10
    That of the rings made such illustrious spoils,
    As Livy[1] has recorded, who errs not,

With those who felt the agony of blows
    By making counterstand to Robert Guiscard,[2]
    And all the rest, whose bones are gathered still   15

At Ceperano, where a renegade
    Was each Apulian, and at Tagliacozzo,[3]
    Where without arms the old Alardo conquered,

And one his limb transpierced, and one lopped off,
　　Should show, it would be nothing to compare　　20
　　With the disgusting mode of the ninth Bolgia.

A cask by losing center-piece or cant
　　Was never shattered so, as I saw one
　　Rent from the chin to where one breaketh wind.

Between his legs were hanging down his entrails;　　25
　　His heart was visible, and the dismal sack
　　That maketh excrement of what is eaten.

While I was all absorbed in seeing him,
　　He looked at me, and opened with his hands
　　His bosom, saying: "See now how I rend me;　　30

How mutilated, see, is Mahomet;
　　In front of me doth Ali[4] weeping go,
　　Cleft in the face from forelock unto chin;

And all the others whom thou here beholdest,
　　Disseminators of scandal and of schism　　35
　　While living were, and therefore are cleft thus.

A devil is behind here, who doth cleave us
　　Thus cruelly, unto the falchion's edge
　　Putting again each one of all this ream,

When we have gone around the doleful road;　　40
　　By reason that our wounds are closed again
　　Ere any one in front of him repass.

But who art thou, that musest on the crag,
　　Perchance to postpone going to the pain
　　That is adjudged upon thine accusations?"　　45

"Nor death hath reached him yet, nor guilt doth bring him,"
　　My Master made reply, "to be tormented;
　　But to procure him full experience,

Me, who am dead, behoves it to conduct him
　　Down here through Hell, from circle unto circle;　　50
　　And this is true as that I speak to thee."

More than a hundred were there when they heard him,
　　Who in the moat stood still to look at me,
　　Through wonderment oblivious of their torture.

"Now say to Fra Dolcino, then, to arm him,　　55
　　Thou, who perhaps wilt shortly see the sun,
　　If soon he wish not here to follow me,

So with provisions, that no stress of snow
　　May give the victory to the Novarese,[5]
　　Which otherwise to gain would not be easy."　　60

After one foot to go away he lifted,
　　This word did Mahomet say unto me,
　　Then to depart upon the ground he stretched it.

Another one, who had his throat pierced through,
　　And nose cut off close underneath the brows,　　65
　　And had no longer but a single ear,

Staying to look in wonder with the others,
　　Before the others did his gullet open,
　　Which outwardly was red in every part,

And said: "O thou, whom guilt doth not condemn,　　70
　　And whom I once saw up in Latian land,
　　Unless too great similitude deceive me,

Call to remembrance Pier da Medicina,
    If e'er thou see again the lovely plain
    That from Vercelli slopes to Marcabò,[6]   75

And make it known to the best two of Fano,
    To Messer Guido and Angiolello likewise,
    That if foreseeing here be not in vain,

Cast over from their vessel shall they be,
    And drowned near unto the Cattolica,[7]   80
    By the betrayal of a tyrant fell.

Between the isles of Cyprus and Majorca[8]
    Neptune ne'er yet beheld so great a crime,
    Neither of pirates nor Argolic people.[9]

That traitor, who sees only with one eye,   85
    And holds the land, which some one here with me
    Would fain be fasting from the vision of,

Will make them come unto a parley with him;
    Then will do so, that to Focara's[10] wind
    They will not stand in need of vow or prayer."   90

And I to him: "Show to me and declare,
    If thou wouldst have me bear up news of thee,
    Who is this person of the bitter vision."

Then did he lay his hand upon the jaw
    Of one of his companions, and his mouth   95
    Oped, crying: "This is he, and he speaks not.

This one, being banished, every doubt submerged
    In Cæsar by affirming the forearmed
    Always with detriment allowed delay."

O how bewildered unto me appeared,   100
    With tongue asunder in his windpipe slit,
    Curio,[11] who in speaking was so bold!

And one, who both his hands dissevered had,
    The stumps uplifting through the murky air,
    So that the blood made horrible his face,   105

Cried out: "Thou shalt remember Mosca[12] also,
    Who said, alas! 'A thing done has an end!'
    Which was an ill seed for the Tuscan people."

"And death unto thy race," thereto I added;
    Whence he, accumulating woe on woe,   110
    Departed, like a person sad and crazed.

But I remained to look upon the crowd;
    And saw a thing which I should be afraid,
    Without some further proof, even to recount,

If it were not that conscience reassures me,   115
    That good companion which emboldens man
    Beneath the hauberk[13] of its feeling pure.

I truly saw, and still I seem to see it,
    A trunk without a head walk in like manner
    As walked the others of the mournful herd.   120

And by the hair it held the head dissevered,
    Hung from the hand in fashion of a lantern,
    And that upon us gazed and said: "O me!"

It of itself made to itself a lamp,
    And they were two in one, and one in two;   125
    How that can be, He knows who so ordains it.

When it was come close to the bridge's foot,
  It lifted high its arm with all the head,
  To bring more closely unto us its words,

Which were: "Behold now the sore penalty,   130
  Thou, who dost breathing go the dead beholding;
  Behold if any be as great as this.

And so that thou may carry news of me,
  Know that Bertram de Born[14] am I, the same
  Who gave to the Young King the evil comfort.   135

I made the father and the son rebellious;
  Achitophel not more with Absalom
  And David[15] did with his accursed goadings.

Because I parted persons so united,
  Parted do I now bear my brain, alas!   140
  From its beginning, which is in this trunk.

Thus is observed in me the counterpoise."

⊰ CANTO XXIX ⊱

Geri del Bello—The Tenth Bolgia: Alchemists—
Griffolino d' Arezzo and Capocchio

THE MANY PEOPLE AND THE DIVERS WOUNDS
These eyes of mine had so inebriated,
That they were wishful to stand still and weep;

But said Virgilius: "What dost thou still gaze at?
　Why is thy sight still riveted down there　　　　　5
　Among the mournful, mutilated shades?

Thou hast not done so at the other Bolge;
　Consider, if to count them thou believest,
　That two-and-twenty miles the valley winds,

And now the moon is underneath our feet;　　　　　10
　Henceforth the time allotted us is brief,
　And more is to be seen than what thou seest."

"If thou hadst," I made answer thereupon,
　"Attended to the cause for which I looked,
　Perhaps a longer stay thou wouldst have pardoned."　15

Meanwhile my Guide departed, and behind him
　I went, already making my reply,
　And superadding: "In that cavern where

I held mine eyes with such attention fixed,
    I think a spirit of my blood laments   20
    The sin which down below there costs so much."

Then said the Master: "Be no longer broken
    Thy thought from this time forward upon him;
    Attend elsewhere, and there let him remain;

For him I saw below the little bridge,   25
    Pointing at thee, and threatening with his finger
    Fiercely, and heard him called Geri del Bello.[1]

So wholly at that time wast thou impeded
    By him who formerly held Altaforte,[2]
    Thou didst not look that way; so he departed."   30

"O my Conductor, his own violent death,
    Which is not yet avenged for him," I said,
    "By any who is sharer in the shame,

Made him disdainful; whence he went away,
    As I imagine, without speaking to me,   35
    And thereby made me pity him the more."

Thus did we speak as far as the first place
    Upon the crag, which the next valley shows
    Down to the bottom, if there were more light.

When we were now right over the last cloister   40
    Of Malebolge, so that its lay-brothers
    Could manifest themselves unto our sight,

Divers lamentings pierced me through and through,
    Which with compassion had their arrows barbed,
    Whereat mine ears I covered with my hands.   45

What pain would be, if from the hospitals
　　Of Valdichiana, 'twixt July and September,
　　And of Maremma and Sardinia[3]

All the diseases in one moat were gathered,
　　Such was it here, and such a stench came from it　　50
　　As from putrescent limbs is wont to issue.

We had descended on the furthest bank
　　From the long crag, upon the left hand still,
　　And then more vivid was my power of sight

Down tow'rds the bottom, where the ministress　　55
　　Of the high Lord, Justice infallible,
　　Punishes forgers, which she here records.

I do not think a sadder sight to see
　　Was in Ægina[4] the whole people sick,
　　(When was the air so full of pestilence,　　60

The animals, down to the little worm,
　　All fell, and afterwards the ancient people,
　　According as the poets have affirmed,

Were from the seed of ants restored again)
　　Than was it to behold through that dark valley　　65
　　The spirits languishing in divers heaps.

This on the belly, that upon the back
　　One of the other lay, and others crawling
　　Shifted themselves along the dismal road.

We step by step went onward without speech,　　70
　　Gazing upon and listening to the sick
　　Who had not strength enough to lift their bodies.

I saw two sitting leaned against each other,
 As leans in heating platter against platter,
 From head to foot bespotted o'er with scabs;   75

And never saw I plied a currycomb[5]
 By stable-boy for whom his master waits,
 Or him who keeps awake unwillingly,

As every one was plying fast the bite
 Of nails upon himself, for the great rage   80
 Of itching which no other succor had.

And the nails downward with them dragged the scab,
 In fashion as a knife the scales of bream,
 Or any other fish that has them largest.

"O thou, that with thy fingers dost dismail thee," 85
 Began my Leader unto one of them,
 "And makest of them pincers now and then,

Tell me if any Latian is with those
 Who are herein; so may thy nails suffice thee
 To all eternity unto this work."   90

"Latians are we, whom thou so wasted seest,
 Both of us here," one weeping made reply;
 "But who art thou, that questionest about us?"

And said the Guide: "One am I who descends
 Down with this living man from cliff to cliff, 95
 And I intend to show Hell unto him."

Then broken was their mutual support,
 And trembling each one turned himself to me,
 With others who had heard him by rebound.

Wholly to me did the good Master gather,   100
    Saying: "Say unto them whate'er thou wishest."
    And I began, since he would have it so:

"So may your memory not steal away
    In the first world from out the minds of men,
    But so may it survive 'neath many suns,   105

Say to me who ye are, and of what people;
    Let not your foul and loathsome punishment
    Make you afraid to show yourselves to me."

"I of Arezzo was," one made reply,
    "And Albert of Siena[6] had me burned;   110
    But what I died for does not bring me here.

'Tis true I said to him, speaking in jest,
    That I could rise by flight into the air,
    And he who had conceit, but little wit,

Would have me show to him the art; and only   115
    Because no Dædalus I made him, made me
    Be burned by one who held him as his son.

But unto the last Bolgia of the ten,
    For alchemy, which in the world I practiced,
    Minos, who cannot err, has me condemned."   120

And to the Poet said I: "Now was ever
    So vain a people as the Sienese?
    Not for a certainty the French by far."

Whereat the other leper, who had heard me,
    Replied unto my speech: "Taking out Stricca,   125
    Who knew the art of moderate expenses,

And Niccolò, who the luxurious use
    Of cloves discovered earliest of all
    Within that garden where such seed takes root;

And taking out the band, among whom squandered   130
    Caccia d'Ascian his vineyards and vast woods,
    And where his wit the Abbagliato[7] proffered!

But, that thou know who thus doth second thee
    Against the Sienese, make sharp thine eye
    Tow'rds me, so that my face well answer thee,   135

And thou shalt see I am Capocchio's[8] shade,
    Who metals falsified by alchemy;
    Thou must remember, if I well descry thee,

How I a skilful ape of nature was."

⊰ CANTO XXX ⊱

Other Falsifiers or Forgers—Gianni Schicchi, Myrrha,
Adam of Brescia, Potiphar's Wife, and Sinon of Troy

'TWAS AT THE TIME WHEN JUNO WAS ENRAGED,
For Semele, against the Theban blood,
As she already more than once had shown,

So reft of reason Athamas became,
 That, seeing his own wife with children twain   5
 Walking encumbered upon either hand,

He cried: "Spread out the nets, that I may take
 The lioness and her whelps upon the passage";
 And then extended his unpitying claws,

Seizing the first, who had the name Learchus,[1]   10
 And whirled him round, and dashed him on a rock;
 And she, with the other burthen, drowned herself—

And at the time when fortune downward hurled
 The Trojan's arrogance, that all things dared,
 So that the king was with his kingdom crushed,   15

Hecuba sad, disconsolate, and captive,
 When lifeless she beheld Polyxena,
 And of her Polydorus on the shore

172

Of ocean was the dolorous one aware,
    Out of her senses like a dog she barked,[2]   20
    So much the anguish had her mind distorted;

But not of Thebes the furies nor the Trojan
    Were ever seen in any one so cruel
    In goading beasts, and much more human members,

As I beheld two shadows pale and naked,   25
    Who, biting, in the manner ran along
    That a boar does, when from the sty turned loose.

One to Capocchio came, and by the nape
    Seized with its teeth his neck, so that in dragging
    It made his belly grate the solid bottom.   30

And the Aretine, who trembling had remained,
    Said to me: "That mad sprite is Gianni Schicchi,
    And raving goes thus harrying other people."

"O," said I to him, "so may not the other
    Set teeth on thee, let it not weary thee   35
    To tell us who it is, ere it dart hence."

And he to me: "That is the ancient ghost
    Of the nefarious Myrrha,[3] who became
    Beyond all rightful love her father's lover.

She came to sin with him after this manner,   40
    By counterfeiting of another's form;
    As he who goeth yonder undertook,

That he might gain the lady of the herd,
    To counterfeit in himself Buoso Donati,[4]
    Making a will and giving it due form."   45

And after the two maniacs had passed
    On whom I held mine eye, I turned it back
    To look upon the other evil-born.

I saw one made in fashion of a lute,
    If he had only had the groin cut off   50
    Just at the point at which a man is forked.

The heavy dropsy, that so disproportions
    The limbs with humors,[5] which it ill concocts,
    That the face corresponds not to the belly,

Compelled him so to hold his lips apart   55
    As does the hectic, who because of thirst
    One tow'rds the chin, the other upward turns.

"O ye, who without any torment are,
    And why I know not, in the world of woe,"
    He said to us, "behold, and be attentive   60

Unto the misery of Master Adam;[6]
    I had while living much of what I wished,
    And now, alas! a drop of water crave.

The rivulets, that from the verdant hills
    Of Cassentin descend down into Arno,   65
    Making their channels to be cold and moist,

Ever before me stand, and not in vain;
    For far more doth their image dry me up
    Than the disease which strips my face of flesh.

The rigid justice that chastizes me   70
    Draweth occasion from the place in which
    I sinned, to put the more my sighs in flight.

There is Romena, where I counterfeited
   The currency imprinted with the Baptist,[7]
   For which I left my body burned above.   75

But if I here could see the tristful soul
   Of Guido, or Alessandro, or their brother,
   For Branda's fount[8] I would not give the sight.

One is within already, if the raving
   Shades that are going round about speak truth;   80
   But what avails it me, whose limbs are tied?

If I were only still so light, that in
   A hundred years I could advance one inch,
   I had already started on the way,

Seeking him out among this squalid folk,   85
   Although the circuit be eleven miles,
   And be not less than half a mile across.

For them am I in such a family;
   They did induce me into coining florins,
   Which had three carats of impurity."[9]   90

And I to him: "Who are the two poor wretches
   That smoke like unto a wet hand in winter,
   Lying there close upon thy right-hand confines?"

"I found them here," replied he, "when I rained
   Into this chasm, and since they have not turned,   95
   Nor do I think they will for evermore.

One the false woman is who accused Joseph,[10]
   The other the false Sinon, Greek of Troy;[11]
   From acute fever they send forth such reek."

And one of them, who felt himself annoyed   100
    At being, peradventure, named so darkly,
    Smote with the fist upon his hardened paunch.

It gave a sound, as if it were a drum;
    And Master Adam smote him in the face,
    With arm that did not seem to be less hard,   105

Saying to him: "Although be taken from me
    All motion, for my limbs that heavy are,
    I have an arm unfettered for such need."

Whereat he answer made: "When thou didst go
    Unto the fire, thou hadst it not so ready: 110
    But hadst it so and more when thou wast coining."

The dropsical: "Thou sayest true in that;
    But thou wast not so true a witness there,
    Where thou wast questioned of the truth at Troy."

"If I spake false, thou falsifiedst the coin,"   115
    Said Sinon; "and for one fault I am here,
    And thou for more than any other demon."

"Remember, perjurer, about the horse,"[12]
    He made reply who had the swollen belly,
    "And rueful be it thee the whole world knows it."   120

"Rueful to thee the thirst be wherewith cracks
    Thy tongue," the Greek said, "and the putrid water
    That hedges so thy paunch before thine eyes."

Then the false-coiner: "So is gaping wide
    Thy mouth for speaking evil, as 'tis wont;   125
    Because if I have thirst, and humor stuff me

Thou hast the burning and the head that aches,
    And to lick up the mirror of Narcissus
    Thou wouldst not want words many to invite thee."

In listening to them was I wholly fixed,   130
    When said the Master to me: "Now just look,
    For little wants it that I quarrel with thee."

When him I heard in anger speak to me,
    I turned me round towards him with such shame
    That still it eddies through my memory.   135

And as he is who dreams of his own harm,
    Who dreaming wishes it may be a dream,
    So that he craves what is, as if it were not;

Such I became, not having power to speak,
    For to excuse myself I wished, and still   140
    Excused myself, and did not think I did it.

"Less shame doth wash away a greater fault,"
    The Master said, "than this of thine has been;
    Therefore thyself disburden of all sadness,

And make account that I am aye beside thee,   145
    If e'er it come to pass that fortune bring thee
    Where there are people in a like dispute;

For a base wish it is to wish to hear it."

⚔ CANTO XXXI ⚔

The Giants, Nimrod, Ephialtes, and Antæus—Descent to Cocytus

ONE AND THE SELFSAME TONGUE FIRST WOUNDED ME,
So that it tinged the one cheek and the other,
And then held out to me the medicine;

Thus do I hear that once Achilles' spear,
 His and his father's, used to be the cause   5
 First of a sad and then a gracious boon.

We turned our backs upon the wretched valley,
 Upon the bank that girds it round about,
 Going across it without any speech.

There it was less than night, and less than day,   10
 So that my sight went little in advance;
 But I could hear the blare of a loud horn,

So loud it would have made each thunder faint,
 Which, counter to it following its way,
 Mine eyes directed wholly to one place.   15

After the dolorous discomfiture
 When Charlemagne the holy emprise lost,
 So terribly Orlando sounded not.[1]

Short while my head turned thitherward I held
    When many lofty towers I seemed to see,   20
    Whereat I: "Master, say, what town is this?"

And he to me: "Because thou peerest forth
    Athwart the darkness at too great a distance,
    It happens that thou errest in thy fancy.

Well shalt thou see, if thou arrivest there,   25
    How much the sense deceives itself by distance;
    Therefore a little faster spur thee on."

Then tenderly he took me by the hand,
    And said: "Before we farther have advanced,
    That the reality may seem to thee   30

Less strange, know that these are not towers, but giants,
    And they are in the well, around the bank,
    From navel downward, one and all of them."

As, when the fog is vanishing away,
    Little by little doth the sight refigure   35
    Whate'er the mist that crowds the air conceals,

So, piercing through the dense and darksome air,
    More and more near approaching tow'rd the verge,
    My error fled, and fear came over me;

Because as on its circular parapets   40
    Montereggione[2] crowns itself with towers,
    E'en thus the margin which surrounds the well

With one half of their bodies turreted
    The horrible giants, whom Jove menaces
    E'en now from out the heavens when he thunders.   45

And I of one already saw the face,
  Shoulders, and breast, and great part of the belly,
  And down along his sides both of the arms.

Certainly Nature, when she left the making
  Of animals like these, did well indeed,   50
  By taking such executors from Mars;

And if of elephants and whales she doth not
  Repent her, whosoever looketh subtly
  More just and more discreet will hold her for it;

For where the argument of intellect   55
  Is added unto evil will and power,
  No rampart can the people make against it.

His face appeared to me as long and large
  As is at Rome the pinecone of Saint Peter's,[3]
  And in proportion were the other bones;   60

So that the margin, which an apron was
  Down from the middle, showed so much of him
  Above it, that to reach up to his hair

Three Frieslanders in vain had vaunted them;
  For I beheld thirty great palms[4] of him   65
  Down from the place where man his mantle buckles.

"Raphael mai amech izabi almi,"[5]
  Began to clamor the ferocious mouth,
  To which were not befitting sweeter psalms.

And unto him my Guide: "Soul idiotic,   70
  Keep to thy horn, and vent thyself with that,
  When wrath or other passion touches thee.

Search round thy neck, and thou wilt find the belt
    Which keeps it fastened, O bewildered soul,
    And see it, where it bars thy mighty breast."   75

Then said to me: "He doth himself accuse;
    This one is Nimrod, by whose evil thought
    One language in the world is not still used.

Here let us leave him and not speak in vain;
    For even such to him is every language   80
    As his to others, which to none is known."

Therefore a longer journey did we make,
    Turned to the left, and a crossbow-shot oft
    We found another far more fierce and large.

In binding him, who might the master be   85
    I cannot say; but he had pinioned close
    Behind the right arm, and in front the other,

With chains, that held him so begirt about
    From the neck down, that on the part uncovered
    It wound itself as far as the fifth gyre.[6]   90

"This proud one wished to make experiment
    Of his own power against the Supreme Jove,"
    My Leader said, "whence he has such a guerdon.[7]

Ephialtes[8] is his name; he showed great prowess.
    What time the giants terrified the gods;   95
    The arms he wielded never more he moves."

And I to him: "If possible, I should wish
    That of the measureless Briareus[9]
    These eyes of mine might have experience."

Whence he replied: "Thou shalt behold Antæus[10]   100
   Close by here, who can speak and is unbound,
   Who at the bottom of all crime shall place us.

Much farther yon is he whom thou wouldst see,
   And he is bound, and fashioned like to this one,
   Save that he seems in aspect more ferocious."   105

There never was an earthquake of such might
   That it could shake a tower so violently,
   As Ephialtes suddenly shook himself.

Then was I more afraid of death than ever,
   For nothing more was needful than the fear,   110
   If I had not beheld the manacles.

Then we proceeded farther in advance,
   And to Antæus came, who, full five ells[11]
   Without the head, forth issued from the cavern.

"O thou, who in the valley fortunate,   115
   Which Scipio the heir of glory made,
   When Hannibal[12] turned back with all his hosts,

Once brought'st a thousand lions for thy prey,
   And who, hadst thou been at the mighty war
   Among thy brothers, some it seems still think   120

The sons of Earth the victory would have gained:
   Place us below, nor be disdainful of it,
   There where the cold doth lock Cocytus[13] up.

Make us not go to Tityus nor Typhœus;[14]
   This one can give of that which here is longed for;   125
   Therefore stoop down, and do not curl thy lip.

Still in the world can he restore thy fame;
    Because he lives, and still expects long life,
    If to itself Grace call him not untimely."

So said the Master; and in haste the other   130
    His hands extended and took up my Guide—
    Hands whose great pressure Hercules once felt.

Virgilius, when he felt himself embraced,
    Said unto me: "Draw nigh, that I may take thee";
    Then of himself and me one bundle made.   135

As seems the Carisenda,[15] to behold
    Beneath the leaning side, when goes a cloud
    Above it so that opposite it hangs;

Such did Antæus seem to me, who stood
    Watching to see him stoop, and then it was   140
    I could have wished to go some other way.

But lightly in the abyss, which swallows up
    Judas with Lucifer, he put us down;
    Nor thus bowed downward made he there delay,

But, as a mast does in a ship, uprose.   145

⊰ CANTO XXXII ⊱

The Ninth Circle: Traitors—The Frozen Lake of Cocytus—
First Division, Caïna: Traitors to Their Kindred—Camicion de'
Pazzi—Second Division, Antenora: Traitors to Their Country—
Dante Questions Bocca degli Abati—Buoso da Duera

IF I HAD RHYMES BOTH ROUGH AND STRIDULOUS,[1]
As were appropriate to the dismal hole
Down upon which thrust all the other rocks,

I would press out the juice of my conception
 More fully; but because I have them not,   5
 Not without fear I bring myself to speak;

For 'tis no enterprise to take in jest,
 To sketch the bottom of all the universe,
 Nor for a tongue that cries Mamma and Babbo.[2]

But may those Ladies[3] help this verse of mine,   10
 Who helped Amphion[4] in enclosing Thebes,
 That from the fact the word be not diverse.

O rabble ill-begotten above all,
 Who're in the place to speak of which is hard,
 'Twere better ye had here been sheep or goats!   15

When we were down within the darksome well,
    Beneath the giant's feet, but lower far,
    And I was scanning still the lofty wall,

I heard it said to me: "Look how thou steppest!
    Take heed thou do not trample with thy feet   20
    The heads of the tired, miserable brothers!"

Whereat I turned me round, and saw before me
    And underfoot a lake, that from the frost
    The semblance had of glass, and not of water.

So thick a veil ne'er made upon its current   25
    In wintertime Danube in Austria,
    Nor there beneath the frigid sky the Don,

As there was here; so that if Tambernich
    Had fallen upon it, or Pietrapana,[5]
    E'en at the edge 'twould not have given a creak.   30

And as to croak the frog doth place himself
    With muzzle out of water—when is dreaming
    Of gleaning oftentimes the peasant-girl—

Livid, as far down as where shame appears,
    Were the disconsolate shades within the ice,   35
    Setting their teeth unto the note of storks.

Each one his countenance held downward bent;
    From mouth the cold, from eyes the doleful heart
    Among them witness of itself procures.

When round about me somewhat I had looked,   40
    I downward turned me, and saw two so close,[6]
    The hair upon their heads together mingled.

"Ye who so strain your breasts together, tell me,"
    I said, "who are you"; and they bent their necks,
    And when to me their faces they had lifted,   45

Their eyes, which first were only moist within,
    Gushed o'er the eyelids, and the frost congealed
    The tears between, and locked them up again.

Clamp never bound together wood with wood
    So strongly; whereat they, like two he-goats,   50
    Butted together, so much wrath o'ercame them.

And one, who had by reason of the cold
    Lost both his ears, still with his visage downward,
    Said: "Why dost thou so mirror thyself in us?

If thou desire to know who these two are,   55
    The valley whence Bisenzio[7] descends
    Belonged to them and to their father Albert.

They from one body came, and all Caïna
    Thou shalt search through, and shalt not find a shade
    More worthy to be fixed in gelatine;   60

Not he in whom were broken breast and shadow
    At one and the same blow by Arthur's hand;
    Focaccia not; not he who me encumbers

So with his head I see no farther forward,
    And bore the name of Sassol Mascheroni;   65
    Well knowest thou who he was, if thou art Tuscan.

And that thou put me not to further speech,
    Know that I Camicion de' Pazzi was,
    And wait Carlino[8] to exonerate me."

Then I beheld a thousand faces, made   70
   Purple with cold; whence o'er me comes a shudder,
   And evermore will come, at frozen ponds.

And while we were advancing tow'rds the middle,
   Where everything of weight unites together,
   And I was shivering in the eternal shade,   75

Whether 'twere will, or destiny, or chance,
   I know not; but in walking 'mong the heads
   I struck my foot hard in the face of one.

Weeping he growled: "Why dost thou trample me?
   Unless thou comest to increase the vengeance   80
   of Montaperti, why dost thou molest me?"

And I: "My Master, now wait here for me,
   That I through him may issue from a doubt;
   Then thou mayst hurry me, as thou shalt wish."

The Leader stopped; and to that one I said   85
   Who was blaspheming vehemently still:
   "Who art thou, that thus reprehendest others?"

"Now who art thou, that goest through Antenora[9]
   Smiting," replied he, "other people's cheeks,
   So that, if thou wert living, 'twere too much?"   90

"Living I am, and dear to thee it may be,"
   Was my response, "if thou demandest fame,
   That 'mid the other notes thy name I place."

And he to me: "For the reverse I long;
   Take thyself hence, and give me no more trouble;   95
   For ill thou knowest to flatter in this hollow."

Then by the scalp behind I seized upon him,
    And said: "It must needs be thou name thyself,
    Or not a hair remain upon thee here."

Whence he to me: "Though thou strip off my hair,   100
    I will not tell thee who I am, nor show thee,
    If on my head a thousand times thou fall."

I had his hair in hand already twisted,
    And more than one shock of it had pulled out,
    He barking, with his eyes held firmly down,   105

When cried another: "What doth ail thee, Bocca?[10]
    Is't not enough to clatter with thy jaws,
    But thou must bark? what devil touches thee?"

"Now," said I, "I care not to have thee speak,
    Accursed traitor; for unto thy shame   110
    I will report of thee veracious news."

"Begone," replied he, "and tell what thou wilt,
    But be not silent, if thou issue hence,
    Of him who had just now his tongue so prompt;

He weepeth here the silver of the French;   115
    'I saw,' thus canst thou phrase it, 'him of Duera[11]
    There where the sinners stand out in the cold.'

If thou shouldst questioned be who else was there,
    Thou hast beside thee him of Beccaria,[12]
    Of whom the gorget Florence slit asunder;   120

Gianni del Soldanier, I think, may be
    Yonder with Ganellon, and Tebaldello[13]
    Who oped Faenza when the people slept."

Already we had gone away from him,
    When I beheld two frozen in one hole,   125
    So that one head a hood was to the other;

And even as bread through hunger is devoured,
    The uppermost on the other set his teeth,
    There where the brain is to the nape united.

Not in another fashion Tydeus[14] gnawed   130
    The temples of Menalippus in disdain,
    Than that one did the skull and the other things.

"O thou, who showest by such bestial sign
    Thy hatred against him whom thou art eating,
    Tell me the wherefore," said I, "with this compact,   135

That if thou rightfully of him complain,
    In knowing who ye are, and his transgression,
    I in the world above repay thee for it,

If that wherewith I speak be not dried up."

⊰ CANTO XXXIII ⊱

Count Ugolino and the Archbishop Ruggieri—The Death of Count Ugolino's Sons—Third Division of the Ninth Circle, Ptolomæa: Traitors to Their Friends—Friar Alberigo, Branco d' Oria

HIS MOUTH UPLIFTED FROM HIS GRIM REPAST,
That sinner, wiping it upon the hair
Of the same head that he behind had wasted.

Then he began: "Thou wilt that I renew
    The desperate grief, which wrings my heart already   5
    To think of only, ere I speak of it;

But if my words be seed that may bear fruit
    Of infamy to the traitor whom I gnaw,
    Speaking and weeping shalt thou see together.

I know not who thou art, nor by what mode   10
    Thou hast come down here; but a Florentine
    Thou seemest to me truly, when I hear thee.

Thou hast to know I was Count Ugolino,
    And this one was Ruggieri[1] the Archbishop;
    Now I will tell thee why I am such a neighbor.   15

That, by effect of his malicious thoughts,
  Trusting in him I was made prisoner,
  And after put to death, I need not say;

But ne'ertheless what thou canst not have heard,
  That is to say, how cruel was my death,   20
  Hear shalt thou, and shalt know if he has wronged me.

A narrow perforation in the mew,²
  Which bears because of me the title of Famine,
  And in which others still must be locked up,

Had shown me through its opening many moons   25
  Already, when I dreamed the evil dream
  Which of the future rent for me the veil.

This one appeared to me as lord and master,
  Hunting the wolf and whelps upon the mountain
  For which the Pisans cannot Lucca see.   30

With sleuth-hounds gaunt, and eager, and well trained,
  Gualandi with Sismondi and Lanfianchi³
  He had sent out before him to the front.

After brief course seemed unto me forespent
  The father and the sons, and with sharp tushes   35
  It seemed to me I saw their flanks ripped open.

When I before the morrow was awake,
  Moaning amid their sleep I heard my sons
  Who with me were, and asking after bread.

Cruel indeed art thou, if yet thou grieve not,   40
  Thinking of what my heart foreboded me,
  And weep'st thou not, what art thou wont to weep at?

They were awake now, and the hour drew nigh
　　At which our food used to be brought to us,
　　And through his dream was each one apprehensive;　45

And I heard locking up the under door
　　Of the horrible tower; whereat without a word
　　I gazed into the faces of my sons.

I wept not, I within so turned to stone;
　　They wept; and darling little Anselm mine　　　　50
　　Said: 'Thou dost gaze so, father, what doth ail thee?'

Still not a tear I shed, nor answer made
　　All of that day, nor yet the night thereafter,
　　Until another sun rose on the world.

As now a little glimmer made its way　　　　　　　55
　　Into the dolorous prison, and I saw
　　Upon four faces my own very aspect,

Both of my hands in agony I bit;
　　And, thinking that I did it from desire
　　Of eating, on a sudden they uprose,　　　　　　60

And said they: 'Father, much less pain 'twill give us
　　If thou do eat of us; thyself didst clothe us
　　With this poor flesh, and do thou strip it off.'

I calmed me then, not to make them more sad.
　　That day we all were silent, and the next.　　　65
　　Ah! obdurate earth, wherefore didst thou not open?

When we had come unto the fourth day, Gaddo
　　Threw himself down outstretched before my feet,
　　Saying, 'My father, why dost thou not help me?'

And there he died; and, as thou seest me,   70
    I saw the three fall, one by one, between
    The fifth day and the sixth; whence I betook me,

Already blind, to groping over each,
    And three days called them after they were dead;
    Then hunger did what sorrow could not do."   75

When he had said this, with his eyes distorted,
    The wretched skull resumed he with his teeth,
    Which, as a dog's, upon the bone were strong.

Ah! Pisa, thou opprobrium of the people
    Of the fair land there where the *Sì* doth sound,[4]   80
    Since slow to punish thee thy neighbors are,

Let the Capraia and Gorgona[5] move,
    And make a hedge across the mouth of Arno
    That every person in thee it may drown!

For if Count Ugolino had the fame   85
    Of having in thy castles thee betrayed,
    Thou shouldst not on such cross have put his sons.

Guiltless of any crime, thou modern Thebes!
    Their youth made Uguccione and Brigata,
    And the other two my song doth name above!   90

We passed still farther onward, where the ice
    Another people ruggedly enswathes,
    Not downward turned, but all of them reversed.

Weeping itself there does not let them weep,
    And grief that finds a barrier in the eyes   95
    Turns itself inward to increase the anguish;

Because the earliest tears a cluster form,
    And, in the manner of a crystal visor,
    Fill all the cup beneath the eyebrow full.

And notwithstanding that, as in a callus,   100
    Because of cold all sensibility
    Its station had abandoned in my face,

Still it appeared to me I felt some wind;
    Whence I: "My Master, who sets this in motion?
    Is not below here every vapor quenched?"   105

Whence he to me: "Full soon shalt thou be where
    Thine eye shall answer make to thee of this,
    Seeing the cause which raineth down the blast."

And one of the wretches of the frozen crust
    Cried out to us: "O souls so merciless   110
    That the last post is given unto you,

Lift from mine eyes the rigid veils, that I
    May vent the sorrow which impregns my heart
    A little, e'er the weeping recongeal."

Whence I to him: "If thou wouldst have me help thee   115
    Say who thou wast; and if I free thee not,
    May I go to the bottom of the ice."

Then he replied: "I am Friar Alberigo;[6]
    He am I of the fruit of the bad garden,
    Who here a date am getting for my fig."   120

"O," said I to him, "now art thou, too, dead?"
    And he to me: "How may my body fare
    Up in the world, no knowledge I possess.

Such an advantage has this Ptolomæa,[7]
 That oftentimes the soul descendeth here   125
 Sooner than Atropos[8] in motion sets it.

And, that thou mayest more willingly remove
 From off my countenance these glassy tears,
 Know that as soon as any soul betrays

As I have done, his body by a demon   130
 Is taken from him, who thereafter rules it,
 Until his time has wholly been revolved.

Itself down rushes into such a cistern;
 And still perchance above appears the body
 Of yonder shade, that winters here behind me. 135

This thou shouldst know, if thou hast just come down;
 It is Ser Branca d' Oria, and many years
 Have passed away since he was thus locked up."

"I think," said I to him, "thou dost deceive me;
 For Branca d' Oria is not dead as yet,   140
 And eats, and drinks, and sleeps, and puts on clothes."

"In moat above," said he, "of Malebranche,
 There where is boiling the tenacious pitch,
 As yet had Michel Zanche[9] not arrived,

When this one left a devil in his stead   145
 In his own body and one near of kin,
 Who made together with him the betrayal.

But hitherward stretch out thy hand forthwith,
 Open mine eyes"—and open them I did not,
 And to be rude to him was courtesy.   150

Ah, Genoese! ye men at variance
    With every virtue, full of every vice
    Wherefore are ye not scattered from the world?

For with the vilest spirit of Romagna
    I found of you one such, who for his deeds   155
    In soul already in Cocytus bathes,

And still above in body seems alive!

⊰ CANTO XXXIV ⊱

*Fourth Division of the Ninth Circle, the Judecca: Traitors to Their
Lords and Benefactors—Lucifer, Judas Iscariot, Brutus, and
Cassius—The Chasm of Lethe—The Ascent*

" '*VEXILLA REGIS PRODEUNT INFERNI*'[1]
Towards us; therefore look in front of thee,"
My Master said, "if thou discernest him."

As, when there breathes a heavy fog, or when
   Our hemisphere is darkening into night,   5
   Appears far off a mill the wind is turning,

Methought that such a building then I saw;
   And, for the wind, I drew myself behind
   My Guide, because there was no other shelter.

Now was I, and with fear in verse I put it,   10
   There where the shades were wholly covered up,
   And glimmered through like unto straws in glass.

Some prone are lying, others stand erect,
   This with the head, and that one with the soles;
   Another, bow-like, face to feet inverts.   15

When in advance so far we had proceeded,
    That it my Master pleased to show to me
    The creature who once had the beauteous semblance,

He from before me moved and made me stop,
    Saying: "Behold Dis,[2] and behold the place   20
    Where thou with fortitude must arm thyself."

How frozen I became and powerless then,
    Ask it not, Reader, for I write it not,
    Because all language would be insufficient.

I did not die, and I alive remained not;   25
    Think for thyself now, hast thou aught of wit,
    What I became, being of both deprived.

The Emperor of the kingdom dolorous[3]
    From his mid-breast forth issued from the ice;
    And better with a giant I compare   30

Than do the giants with those arms of his;
    Consider now how great must be that whole,
    Which unto such a part conforms itself.

Were he as fair once, as he now is foul,
    And lifted up his brow against his Maker,   35
    Well may proceed from him all tribulation.

O, what a marvel it appeared to me,
    When I beheld three faces on his head!
    The one in front, and that vermilion was;

Two were the others, that were joined with this   40
    Above the middle part of either shoulder,
    And they were joined together at the crest;

And the right-hand one seemed 'twixt white and yellow;
    The left was such to look upon as those
    Who come from where the Nile falls valley-ward.   45

Underneath each came forth two mighty wings,
    Such as befitting were so great a bird;
    Sails of the sea I never saw so large.

No feathers had they, but as of a bat
    Their fashion was; and he was waving them,   50
    So that three winds proceeded forth therefrom.

Thereby Cocytus wholly was congealed.
    With six eyes did he weep, and down three chins
    Trickled the teardrops and the bloody drivel.

At every mouth he with his teeth was crunching   55
    A sinner, in the manner of a brake,
    So that he three of them tormented thus.

To him in front the biting was as naught
    Unto the clawing, for sometimes the spine
    Utterly stripped of all the skin remained.   60

"That soul up there which has the greatest pain,"
    The Master said, "is Judas Iscariot;
    With head inside, he plies his legs without.

Of the two others, who head downward are,
    The one who hangs from the black jowl is Brutus;   65
    See how he writhes himself, and speaks no word.

And the other, who so stalwart seems, is Cassius.[4]
    But night is reascending,[5] and 'tis time
    That we depart, for we have seen the whole."

As seemed him good, I clasped him round the neck,   70
    And he the vantage seized of time and place,
    And when the wings were opened wide apart,

He laid fast hold upon the shaggy sides;
    From fell to fell descended downward then
    Between the thick hair and the frozen crust.   75

When we were come to where the thigh revolves
    Exactly on the thickness of the haunch,
    The Guide, with labor and with hard-drawn breath,

Turned round his head where he had had his legs,
    And grappled to the hair, as one who mounts,   80
    So that to Hell I thought we were returning.

"Keep fast thy hold, for by such stairs as these,"
    The Master said, panting as one fatigued,
    "Must we perforce depart from so much evil."

Then through the opening of a rock he issued,   85
    And down upon the margin seated me;
    Then tow'rds me he outstretched his wary step.

I lifted up mine eyes and thought to see
    Lucifer in the same way I had left him;
    And I beheld him upward hold his legs.   90

And if I then became disquieted,
    Let stolid people think who do not see
    What the point is beyond which I had passed.

"Rise up," the Master said, "upon thy feet;
    The way is long, and difficult the road,   95
    And now the sun to middle-tierce returns."

It was not any palace corridor
   There where we were, but dungeon natural,
   With floor uneven and unease of light.

"Ere from the abyss I tear myself away,   100
   My Master," said I when I had arisen,
   "To draw me from an error speak a little;

Where is the ice? and how is this one fixed
   Thus upside down? and how in such short time
   From eve to morn has the sun made his transit?"   105

And he to me: "Thou still imaginest
   Thou art beyond the center, where I grasped
   The hair of the fell worm, who mines the world.

That side thou wast, so long as I descended;
   When round I turned me, thou didst pass the point 110
   To which things heavy draw from every side,[6]

And now beneath the hemisphere art come
   Opposite that which overhangs the vast
   Dry-land, and 'neath whose cope was put to death

The Man who without sin was born and lived.   115
   Thou hast thy feet upon the little sphere
   Which makes the other face of the Judecca.[7]

Here it is morn when it is evening there;
   And he who with his hair a stairway made us
   Still fixed remaineth as he was before.   120

Upon this side he fell down out of heaven;
   And all the land, that whilom here emerged,[8]
   For fear of him made of the sea a veil,

And came to our hemisphere; and peradventure
    To flee from him, what on this side appears   125
    Left the place vacant here, and back recoiled."

A place there is below, from Beelzebub[9]
    As far receding as the tomb extends,
    Which not by sight is known, but by the sound

Of a small rivulet, that there descendeth   130
    Through chasm within the stone, which it has gnawed
    With course that winds about and slightly falls.

The Guide and I into that hidden road
    Now entered, to return to the bright world;
    And without care of having any rest   135

We mounted up, he first and I the second,
    Till I beheld through a round aperture
    Some of the beauteous things that Heaven doth bear;

Thence we came forth to rebehold the stars.

ENDNOTES

INTRODUCTION

1. Dante Alighieri, *La Vita Nuova*, trans. Barbara Reynolds (London: Penguin, 2004), 64.
2. Joan M. Ferrante, *The Political Vision of the "Divine Comedy"* (Princeton: Princeton University Press, 1984), 83.
3. Erich Auerbach, *Dante: Poet of the Secular World,* trans. Ralph Mannheim (Chicago: University of Chicago Press, 1961), 175.

CANTO I

1. (p. 1) *Midway upon the journey of our life:* At Easter 1300, around which time the poem is set, Dante was thirty-five years old—exactly halfway through the normal human life span of seventy years, as defined by the Bible: "three score years and ten" (Psalms 90:10).
2 (p. 2) *panther:* This creature (which is more commonly referred to as a leopard in translation) may represent physical lust, the unbridled desire of pleasure—variable, unpredictable, outrunning moral restraint. One political interpretation concerning this animal is that its "spotted skin" may be representative of Florence, which was at the time divided by factions—the Black Guelfs and the White Guelfs.
3. (p. 2) *lion's aspect:* Like the panther, the lion may signify a second misleading desire threatening to overpower the soul—in this case, probably the lust for fame. In terms of politics, the lion may be representative of the royal house of France (it was French troops who occupied Florence and secured it for the Black Guelfs, which led to Dante's exile).
4. (p. 3) *she-wolf:* The she-wolf, the most dangerous creature blocking Dante's path, is the embodiment of ravenous, insatiable avarice, the overwhelming desire to possess. In a political interpretation, she may be the symbol of the contemporary, rapacious papacy.
5. (p. 3) *did one present himself:* This is the classical Roman poet, Virgil (70–19 BCE), author of the *Aeneid* and the *Georgics,* and for Dante, the supreme

model of poetic style and insight, as well as the wisest of guides—within human limitations. From this point in the narrative, Virgil is Dante's escort through the *Inferno* and up onto the mountain of Purgatory, though not being a Christian, Virgil cannot continue with him to ascend into Paradise.

6. (p. 3) Sub Julio . . . *under the good Augustus . . . false and lying gods: Sub Julio* means "under Julius." Virgil was born during the lifetime of Julius Caesar (ca. 100–44 BCE) and lived on into the reign of Emperor Augustus (d. 14 CE); "the time of false and lying gods" refers to the fact that Rome was pagan during this period.

7. (p. 4) *Son of Anchises . . . Ilion the superb was burned:* Aeneas was the son of Anchises; a prince of Troy (Ilion), Aeneas escaped the burning city, and his descendants, according to legend, founded Rome.

8. (p. 5) *the Greyhound:* The Greyhound is the antitype of the she-wolf, probably a righteous ruler who desires no additional riches or land but rather is solely intent on restoring justice to the world. It is not clear which historical figure the Greyhound represents but, as revealed in other writings, Dante was hopeful that the German king Henry VII would bring about order and peace to Italy, which the ruler entered in 1310. Henry VII became Holy Roman emperor in 1312 but accomplished little before his premature death in 1313. Another possibility is that the Greyhound represents one of Dante's hosts in exile—Verona ruler Cangrande della Scala, whose name means "big dog."

9. (p. 5) *'Twixt Feltro and Feltro:* This reference has long puzzled Dante commentators. Longfellow's use of capital letters here implies that "Feltro and Feltro" are names of places (Feltre and Montefeltre in northern Italy), thus suggesting that this is the area from which the righteous ruler will come. For Longfellow, therefore, this suggests Cangrande della Scala (see previous note), ruler of Verona, which lies in the region indicated. Alternative interpretations revolve around *feltro* as a common noun. These include *feltro* defined as "coarse cloth," to refer to the garb of a holy friar untouched by materialism; someone born under the sign of the Twins, Castor and Pollux, who wear headgear made of *feltro*, meaning "felt"; a reference to the felt-lined urns used to collect votes for magistrates, which would suggest an elective ruler; or a reference to a technical aspect of paper making, in which new paper was dried between felts, signifying the public, written laws that the righteous ruler would enforce.

10. (p. 5) *Camilla . . . Euryalus, Turnus, Nisus:* Roman heroes who died for their homeland.

11. (p. 5) *With her . . . I will leave thee:* The "her" to whom Virgil refers was, in life, Beatrice Portinari (1266–1290), whom Dante worshipped from afar in chaste, unrequited love, from the age of nine when he first saw her (she was eight at the time). Beatrice died when she was only twenty-four. In Dante's *Comedy*, she resides in Paradise and expresses the height of

Christian wisdom. In some allegorical interpretations, she is Faith, as Virgil is Reason, though others argue neither are mere ciphers, as they are fully imagined as characters in the poetic narrative.

CANTO II

1. (p. 7) *Silvius the parent:* In the *Aeneid*, Aeneas, father of Silvius, visited the underworld while still alive.
2. (p. 8) *I not Æneas am, I am not Paul:* Just as Aeneas visited the underworld, Saint Paul, according to legend rather than the Bible, journeyed through Hell with an angelic guide. Saint Paul's journey was retold in many versions and languages, the earliest being from the fourth century. The story is often seen as a key precursor to the *Comedy*.
3. (p. 10) *the lesser circles:* Heaven—Paradiso—was envisaged as a series of ascending spheres (here circles), the highest being the empyrean, in which dwells God. Dante is suggesting here that Beatrice is at the head of humanity in her proximity to the highest spheres.
4. (p. 10) *gentle Lady:* The Virgin Mary.
5. (p. 10) *Lucia:* Saint Lucy (ca. 283–304), an early Christian who was martyred when she refused to marry a pagan nobleman. She is one of the seven women, apart from the Virgin Mary, mentioned in the Canon of the Mass.
6. (p. 11) *Rachel:* Wife of Jacob, and mother of Joseph and Benjamin, in the Old Testament.
7. (p. 11) *benedight:* Blessed.

CANTO III

1. (p. 13) *dolent:* Grievous.
2. (p. 14) *caitiff:* Captive.
3. (p. 16) *Acheron:* One of the rivers of Hell.
4. (p. 16) *Charon:* The ferryman who, in classical myth, transports souls across the river into the underworld.
5. (p. 17) *glede:* Cinders or embers.
6. (p. 18) *champaign:* Open countryside.

CANTO IV

1. (p. 20) *The foremost circle that surrounds the abyss:* Limbo, in effect an antechamber to Hell proper; there dwell the virtuous who did not know Christ and, thus, could not be redeemed.
2. (p. 21), *the First Parent:* Adam, the first man.
3. (p. 22) *Homer . . . Horace . . . Ovid . . . Lucan:* The four greatest poets: Homer, foundational poet of Greek literature, along with Horace, Ovid, and Lucan, the leading Roman authors.

4. (p. 24) *Electra . . . Saladin:* Electra, mother of Dardanus—founder of Troy; Hector, prince of Troy; Aeneas, prince of Troy, whose descendants founded Rome; Caesar, as in Julius Caesar, who brought the Roman republic to an end; Camilla, a legendary woman warrior who fought against Aeneas in Italy; Penthesilea, queen of the Amazons, who fought for Troy; Latinus, king of Latium in central Italy; Brutus, the man who deposed Tarquin—the last king of Rome (not the Brutus who assassinated Caesar); Lucretia, a virtuous Roman woman who was raped by Tarquin's son; Julia, daughter of Julius Caesar; Marcia, wife of Cato the Younger (who, uniquely for a pagan, makes it into Dante's *Purgatory*); Cornelia, either daughter of Scipio Africanus the Elder, or Caesar's wife—either way, an exemplary Roman matron; Saladin, the Kurd who became sultan of Egypt and Syria and was more of a model of chivalry in tales of the Crusades than any of his Christian enemies.

5. (p. 24) *Socrates . . . Plato . . . Democritus . . . Diogenes . . . Anaxagoras . . . Thales . . . Zeno . . . Empedocles . . . Heraclitus:* Ancient Greek philosophers.

6. (p. 24) *Dioscorides . . . the great Comment made:* Dioscorides, a Greek botanist; Orpheus, legendary poet who himself descended into the underworld; Tully, meaning Cicero (Tully was a clan name), the great Roman moral philosopher and statesman; Livy, Roman writer and historian; Seneca, Roman philosopher; Euclid, Greek mathematician; Ptolemy, Greek cosmologist; Galen and Hippocrates, Greek medical theorists; Avicenna and Averroes, Arab philosophers whose writings encapsulated much of the philosophy of Aristotle (translations of their works made Aristotle's philosophy known in the West). "The great Comment" refers to Averroes' commentary on Aristotle.

CANTO V

1. (p. 25) *Minos:* In the underworld of Virgil's *Aeneid*, Minos was the judge who assessed souls and determined their final destination. He serves the same purpose here, possessing a tail that coils itself around a soul in judgment, the number of times indicating to which circle of Hell the soul is to be consigned. (In Greek mythology, this same Minos was the king of Crete, under whose palace at Knossos lay the Labyrinth and its inhabitant, the Minotaur—a creature bearing a bull's head and a man's body.)

2. (p. 27) *Semiramis . . . Ninus . . . Sichæus . . . Cleopatra . . . Helen . . . Achilles . . . Paris . . . Tristan:* Those who abandoned themselves, and the fate of their souls, to love. Semiramis was a queen of Assyria, widow of Ninus, who founded Nineveh; the widow of Sichaeus is Dido, queen of Carthage, who killed herself when abandoned by her lover, Aeneas; Cleopatra, queen of Egypt, made political hay while the romantic sun shone, first with Julius Caesar and then Mark Antony; Helen, wife of Menelaus, whose kidnapping by Paris of Troy, and then willing relationship with her captor, began the Trojan war; Achilles, the

semidivine Greek hero who was killed in the Trojan War—with a twist in some versions, alluded to here, that he was undone by falling in love with Polyxena, daughter of King Priam of Troy; Paris, prince of Troy and seducer of Helen; Tristan, whose love of Isolde, wife of King Mark of Cornwall, brought destruction down upon them.

3. (p. 28) *incarnadine:* Bloodred.

4. (p. 28) *the city:* The city is Ravenna, and the speaker is Francesca, who was murdered in the late thirteenth century by her husband, Gianciotto Malatesta, lord of Rimini, when he discovered her adulterous affair with his brother, Paolo, whom he also killed.

5. (p. 29) *Caina:* Later in the *Inferno* we discover that Caina is the first ring of the ninth circle; named after Cain (who killed his brother, Abel), this ring is reserved for murderers of family members.

6. (p. 30) *Galeotto:* In the King Arthur romances, Galeotto (also known as Gallehault or Galehaut) acted as the go-between for his friend Sir Lancelot and Guinevere in the couple's adulterous affair—just as here the storybook brought together Paolo and Francesca.

CANTO VI

1. (p. 31) *Cerberus:* The monstrous, three-headed dog who guards Hell in classical mythology; here, he is stationed in the third circle of Hell.

2. (p. 33) *Ciacco:* A Florentine nicknamed "Ciacco," which means "hog."

3. (p. 33) *the divided city . . . him who now is on the coast:* Italy had long been divided into two broad factions: the Ghibellines (who initially supported the emperor) and the Guelfs (who initially supported the pope). However, these larger allegiances were almost entirely fluid, depending on changing interests and local political contexts. In the latter part of the thirteenth century, the Guelfs of Florence ("the divided city") had themselves split into two factions: the Black Guelfs and the White Guelfs. In 1300, when the *Comedy* is set, the Whites dominated, but they would be overthrown the following year, due to the conspiring of Pope Boniface VIII (the person here referred to as being "on the coast") with the Blacks.

4. (p. 34) *The just are two:* The identities of the "two" are not known for certain, but they may be Dante himself and either his friend Guido Cavalcanti or Giano della Bella, the latter having reformed the laws of Florence.

5. (p. 34) *Farinata and Tegghiaio . . . Jacopo Rusticucci, Arrigo, and Mosca:* Farinata degli Uberti, a Ghibelline faction fighter in mid-thirteenth-century Florence; Tegghiaio Aldobrandi and Jacopo Rusticucci (who are found among the sodomites in canto 16), Florentine noblemen of the mid-thirteenth century, also caught up in the factional politics of the city; Arrigo, possibly Oderigo dei Fifanti, and Mosca dei Lamberti—both of whom took actions leading to a murder in a marriage dispute between

families in 1215, which set off the faction fighting that would continue to tear Florence apart during Dante's time.

CANTO VII

1. (p. 36) *Papë Satàn, Papë Satàn, Aleppë!:*[1] These words spoken by Plutus (the classical god of wealth, who here oversees the fourth circle and its souls condemned for avarice) are clearly an appeal to Satan, but there is no further detectable meaning or sense in them.

2. (p. 36) *Michael:* The archangel Michael, who overcame the rebellious angels led by Satan.

3. (p. 37) *Charybdis:* In classical mythology, a monster who, along with Scylla, guarded the straits of Messina, where waves—and sometimes ships—would break upon the rocks.

CANTO VIII

1. (p. 43) *Phlegyas:* Phlegyas is another boatman, here ferrying the condemned across the Styx. In Greek mythology, he was the half-human son of Ares. He destroyed the temple of Apollo—not a good move—when that god was threatening to carry off his daughter; as a result, Phlegyas made a quick descent to the underworld.

2. (p. 43) *For thee I know:* This is Philippo (sometimes spelled Filippo) Argenti, a Florentine near-contemporary of Dante, who was renowned for his arrogance. His family belonged to the Black Guelf faction and was bitterly opposed to Dante's return from exile. In this episode, whatever his larger purposes, Dante also seems to be settling a personal score.

3. (p. 44) *Dis:* In Roman mythology, Dis was another name for the underworld itself, as well as for the god who ruled the underworld. Here, it indicates the lower circles of Hell, which are occupied by those sinners who deliberately pursued evil—as opposed to those in the upper circles, who were weak rather than malicious and, therefore, less culpable.

CANTO IX

1. (p. 49) *Erictho:* A witch who could conjure souls from the dead to foretell the future.

2. (p. 49) *Erinnys:* Erinnys (a variant spelling of Erinyes) is another name for the Furies—snake-clad daughters of the night, embodying vengeance.

3. (p. 50) *Medusa:* The Gorgon Medusa, with snakes writhing for hair, turned to stone all those who looked upon her, the figure of despair.

4. (p. 50) *Theseus:* The Athenian king Theseus entered the underworld to try to carry off Persephone (queen of the underworld) on behalf of a friend, who wanted her for his wife. Theseus failed but was rescued by Hercules.

5. (p. 51) *one sent from Heaven:* Probably the archangel Michael.

6. (p. 52) *Arles . . . Pola:* Arles (in southern France) and Pola (on the coast of modern Croatia) were famous burial grounds.

CANTO X

1. (p. 55) *Farinata:* Farinata degli Uberti, a Florentine himself, fought against Florence, winning the Battle of Montaperti in 1260, and was urged on to destroy the city. He refused to do so. After his death, he was declared a heretic, and his bones were disinterred from sacred ground.
2. (p. 56) *a shadow at his side . . . Guido:* This is another heretic, Cavalcante dei Cavalcanti, the father of Dante's old friend Guido Cavalcanti. Dante says Guido held Virgil "in disdain," presumably rejecting him as the model poet.
3. (p. 57) *the Arbia:* The torrent Arbia, near Siena, stained by crimson blood from the Battle of Montaperti.
4. (p. 58) *the second Frederick and the Cardinal:* Emperor Frederick II (1194–1250), referred to as *stupor mundi* ("astonishment of the world"), ruler of Sicily and Naples and, as Holy Roman emperor, titular overlord of Germany, where he also controlled vast lands. He was widely viewed as a heretic—a religious skeptic, tolerant of Muslims—and he was excommunicated by the pope for failing to execute a vow to pursue the Sixth Crusade. The Cardinal is Ottaviano degli Ubaldini (d. 1273), who was at the forefront of Italy's factional feuds.

CANTO XI

1. (p. 60) *Pope Anastasius . . . Photinus:* Anastasius II was a fifth-century pope, reputed to have denied the divine nature of Christ, as he welcomed Photinus, bishop of Sirmium (in modern Serbia), who espoused that doctrine.
2. (p. 61) *games:* Gambles.
3. (p. 62) *barrators:* A barrator is a vexatious litigant—someone who stirs up disputes.
4. (p. 64) *usurer:* A usurer is one who makes money out of money—through charging interest. Though now at the core of Western civilization, usury was condemned (though already widely practiced) in Dante's time; it was regarded as an attempt to breed something from nothing, sterile, inimical to the possibility of creativity that God had bestowed on human beings.
5. (p. 64) *Fishes on the horizon . . . over Caurus lies:* Pisces is rising in the east, and the Wain (meaning Ursa Major) is in the northwestern part of the sky, as indicated by the fact that it is "over Caurus," the northwestern wind—in other words, it is four o'clock in the morning on Holy Saturday.

CANTO XII

1. (p. 65) *Trent, the Adige:* Trent, a city in the Italian Dolomites, in the valley of the Adige River.

2. (p. 65) *The infamy of Crete:* The Minotaur.
3. (p. 66) *the Duke of Athens:* Theseus.
4. (p. 66) *supernal:* Pertaining to Heaven.
5. (p. 68) *Chiron . . . Nessus . . . Dejanira . . . Pholus:* Chiron, Nessus, and Pholus were centaurs—mythical creatures said to be part man, part horse. Chiron was tutor to Achilles; Nessus was killed by Hercules, for his attempted rape of Hercules' wife Dejanira; Pholus was a friend of Hercules.
6. (p. 68) *Some one:* Beatrice.
7. (p. 69) *Alexander . . . Dionysius:* Alexander the Great, who conquered most of the known world. Dionysius, tyrant of Syracuse.
8. (p. 69) *Azzolin:* Ezzolino da Romano, Ghibelline mainstay of Emperor Frederick II in northern Italy, and later his son-in-law.
9. (p. 69) *Obizzo:* Obizzo II d'Este, Guelf warrior and Marquess of Ferrara; he was reputed to have been murdered in 1293 by his son, here referred to as his stepson.
10. (p. 69) *A shade . . . is honored:* The shade is Guy de Montfort, who in 1271 in Viterbo (near Rome), murdered Prince Henry, nephew of the English king Henry III, in revenge for the death of his father, Simon de Montfort, who had been killed during a baronial rebellion against the king. The dead prince was memorialized by a statue, located upon the Thames in London, holding a casket with his heart inside.
11. (p. 70) *Attila . . . Pyrrhus . . . Sextus . . . Rinier da Corneto and Rinier Pazzo:* Attila the Hun (d. 453 CE), scourge of the Roman Empire in its dying years; Pyrrhus, either the violent son of Achilles, or the king of Epirus who invaded Italy; Sextus (ca. 67–35 BCE), son of Pompey, who fought a pirate war against Rome; Rinier da Corneto and Rinier Pazzo, both thirteenth-century brigands—the former terrorized the Maremma on the Tuscan coast, and the latter wreaked havoc in the territory southeast of Florence.

CANTO XIII

1. (p. 71) *Cecina and Corneto:* Towns on the edge of the Maremma marshlands.
2. (p. 71) *the hideous Harpies:* In classical mythology, a harpy was a monster bearing the form of a bird of prey, with huge talons and the head of a woman.
3. (p. 73) *I am the one:* This is Pier della Vigna, born around 1190, chancellor and chief adviser to Emperor Frederick II. However, he lost Frederick's trust; accused of conspiracy, he was imprisoned and blinded. In 1249, he committed suicide by beating his own brains out against a wall.
4. (p. 73) *Cæsar . . . Augustus:* Both names are used here to refer to Emperor Frederick II.
5. (p. 76) *And two behold! . . . . O Jacopo,:* The first of the "two" is Lano, an extravagant man about town in Siena, who died in the 1280s at Pieve del Toppo in a battle against Arezzo—a battle in which Dante himself fought.

The second is Jacopo di Sant'Andrea (d. 1239), who, the story went, was merely amused when his property was consumed by flames.

6. (p. 76) *Who wast thou:* It is not certain to whom Virgil is speaking and who in turn goes on to speak; the unknown individual is probably a Florentine whose career foundered in the 1290s—a description that could apply to numerous figures.

7. (p. 76) *that city . . . its first patron . . . the ashes left by Attila:* Florence's first patron in pre-Christian times was Mars. His statue was thrown in the Arno when the city was sacked in 542 CE—by Totila, not by Attila— but it was retrieved from the river and reerected; ultimately it was destroyed by a flood in 1333. The unknown speaker is reflecting that Florence, beset by internecine violence, continues to be influenced by Mars.

CANTO XIV

1. (p. 77) *arid and thick sand . . . Cato:* Cato, in resistance to Julius Caesar, led the defeated army of Pompey across "the arid and thick sand" of the Sahara.

2. (p. 78) *As Alexander, in those torrid parts of India:* A reference to Alexander the Great's invasion of north India.

3. (p. 78) *gleeds:* Cinders.

4. (p. 79) *Mongibello . . . Vulcan . . . Phlegra:* Mongibello is Mount Etna, where the Roman god of fire, Vulcan, who was also associated with the making of arms and iron, was said to have his forge. Phlegra is the battlefield in Greece where the gods defeated the giants.

5. (p. 79) *Capaneus . . . Thebes besieged:* Capaneus was the most impulsive of the Seven against Thebes, the legendary seven chieftains who died in an assault on the city of Thebes. While scaling the city walls, Capaneus yelled defiance at Jupiter—who struck him dead with a thunderbolt.

6. (p. 80) *Bulicamë:* An area near Viterbo in which a spa grew up around a sulphurous spring. One stream leading away from it had prostitutes' huts lining its banks.

7. (p. 80) *king:* Cronus—in Roman mythology, Saturn—king of the Titans and father of Zeus.

8. (p. 81) *Rhea:* Greek goddess who hid her son Zeus in a cave on Mount Ida, because her brother/husband, Cronus, would devour any child he fathered out of fear that one of them would overthrow him.

9. (p. 81) *A grand old man:* A reference to the "great image" that came to Nebuchadnezzar in a dream. From the gold of his head, he is made of progressively lesser materials, down to the clay of his right foot; his composition may signify the gradual decline of civilization from its golden age beginnings. His tears—which fall down his body into the rivers of the underworld and continue down to that realm's lowest point at the core of the earth—may be the accumulated evils of human beings.

10. (p. 81) *Acheron, Styx, and Phlegethon . . . Cocytus:* Acheron, Styx, and Phlegethon are three rivers of Hell, with the final stream, Cocytus, becoming the frozen lake at its deepest point.

11. (p. 82) *Lethe and Phlegethon:* Lethe is the river of forgetfulness, at the summit of the mountain of Purgatory. Phlegethon is the river seething with blood, encountered in canto 12.

CANTO XV

1. (p. 83) *'twixt Cadsand and Bruges . . . the Paduans along the Brenta . . . Chiarentana feel the heat:* Dante is referring to the sea dykes along the coast north of Calais (Cadsand) up the Flemish coast toward Bruges, and to the embankments along the Brenta River in the region of Padua, located in northern Italy. Chiarentana was a territory in the mountains to the north, from where flood water came when the heat of the spring sun melted the ice.

2. (p. 84) *Ser Brunetto:* Brunetto Latini (ca. 1220–1294), a mentor or tutor of Dante, or maybe even his guardian after the death of Dante's father. Latini was a notary, scholar, orator, and diplomat. He was also an exponent of Cicero as a guide in public affairs, which became increasingly important in Florence as one of the foundations of the Renaissance. He persuaded Dante to read Boethius after the death of Beatrice, an act that suggests an emotional closeness between the two.

3. (p. 85) *Fesole:* A city in the hills just above Florence. Dante believed that the divisions among the Florentines could be traced back to "immigrants" from Fiesole (here, Fesole) intermarrying with the original stock of the Romans who had founded Florence.

4. (p. 85) *crabbed sorbs:* The bitter fruits of the service tree.

5. (p. 87) *Priscian . . . Francis of Accorso:* Priscian, around 500 CE, wrote a Latin grammar, which became standard in medieval schools. Francis d'Accorso (ca. 1182–ca. 1260) was a lawyer from Bologna University, who wrote a great compilation of commentaries on Roman law.

6. (p. 87) *That one, who by the Servant of the Servants . . . to Bacchiglione:* The "Servant of the Servants of God" refers to the pope. In 1295, Pope Boniface VIII demoted the bishop of Florence, Andrea dei Mozzi, transferring him from that city (located on the banks of the Arno River) to the lesser see of Vicenza, a city on the River Bacchiglione.

7. (p. 87) *Tesoro:* Brunetto Latini's *Li Livres dou Trésor,* written in exile in France, was not only an encyclopedia, but his masterwork. Dante made great use of it.

8. (p. 87) *Green Mantle:* Every year a celebrated race was run in Verona, with the prizes being green cloths.

CANTO XVI

1. (p. 89) *He was . . . his sword:* Guido Guerra (grandson of Gualdrada—a Florentine noblewoman, famed for her beauty and virtue) was a Florentine

nobleman and Guelf, who made his reputation fighting against the Ghibellines of Arezzo. He had advised against the attack on Siena that led to the Battle of Montaperti in 1260; at that battle, the Ghibellines temporarily triumphed, resulting in Guido's exile from Florence.

2. (p. 89) *Tegghiaio Aldobrandi:* Like Guido Guerra, Tegghiaio Aldobrandi advised against the attack on Siena that led to the Battle of Montaperti.

3. (p. 90) *Jacopo Rusticucci:* Jacopo Rusticucci is the speaker. He was a nobleman involved in Florentine faction fighting in the mid-thirteenth century, but the historical reason for his appearance in this region of Hell is unknown. Whereas others in this section have likely been condemned for sodomy, he may have been guilty of bestiality. The term translated by Longfellow as "savage" may be a noun, *fiera,* meaning "wild animal."

4. (p. 91) *Guglielmo Borsier:* A Florentine, probably an aristocrat, who died in 1300. His surname means "purse-maker."

5. (p. 92) *that stream . . . San Benedetto:* Dante is describing here (not very accurately) the area to the north of Tuscany, as the Apennines extend into what is now Emilia-Romagna.

6. (p. 92) *I had a cord . . . panther:* Possibly Dante's cord is a friar's girdle, given that he may have hoped, through Franciscan self-discipline, to withstand lust—represented by the panther, one of the three beasts Dante encountered when lost in the dark wood in canto 1.

CANTO XVII

1. (p. 94) *the monster with the pointed tail:* This is Geryon. In Greek mythology, he was a monster with three heads (or bodies). Here, he has the face of a "just man" (a fraudulent display, since in reality, he is a monster), the body of a reptile, and a scorpionlike tail with a venomous sting. And, vitally for Dante and Virgil, he can fly and transport them to the lower regions of Hell.

2. (p. 96) *blazon . . . a lion . . . a goose:* By these heraldic emblems, or blazons—the lion, the goose—their families are recognized.

3. (p. 96) *an azure sow and gravid:* Here, the heraldic emblem of the sow is "gravid" (i.e., pregnant). The symbol is that of Rinaldo Scrovegni, renowned as a moneylender in Padua. Moneylenders (usurers) were viewed as economically barren, trying to breed money from money, spurning God-given creativity and real increase. (Similarly, sodomites were regarded as sexually barren, which is why they and usurers are grouped together in the same circle of Hell.) Rinaldo's son, Enrico Scrovegni, built the Arena Chapel in Padua, in expiation of his father's sins as a usurer; the structure features frescoes by Giotto, and is now traditionally regarded as one of the foundational works of modern art.

4. (p. 97) *quartan:* A quartan fever is one with a crisis recurring every fourth day.

5. (p. 98) *Phaeton:* Phaeton was the son of Helios, the Greek sun god. He drove his father's chariot and lost control, putting the earth at risk of

being consumed by flames. Zeus killed Phaeton with a thunderbolt in order to put a stop to the destruction.

6. (p. 98) *Icarus:* In Greek mythology, Icarus was the son of Daedalus, the great craftsman. Icarus flew too close to the sun on waxen wings made by his father; this action caused the wings to melt, and Icarus plunged to his death in the sea.

CANTO XVIII

1. (p. 100) *Malebolge:* Malebolge means "evil ditches," which make up the seventh circle of Dante's Hell.

2. (p. 101) *Bolgia:* Bolgia, the singular of *bolge*, refers to a ditch—one of the ten making up this region of Hell.

3. (p. 101) *The year of Jubilee:* The year 1300 was declared a year of jubilee by the pope, and Rome was filled with pilgrims, heading across the Tiber River, by bridge, to the shrine of Saint Peter.

4. *(p. 102) Venedico Caccianimico . . . pungent sauces:* Venedico Caccianimico was a leading figure of Bologna, near which there was a place of execution bearing a name much like the phrase "pungenti salse," translated by Longfellow as "pungent sauces." Venedico tells here of his pimping of his sister, Ghisola, to Obizzo II d'Este.

5. (p. 103) *That Jason is . . . Colchians of the Ram . . . Lemnos . . . Hypsipyle . . . also for Medea is vengeance done:* In Greek mythology, Jason—leader of the Argonauts—stole the golden fleece (of the Ram) from the Colchians. He is condemned here for seducing Hypsipyle on the island of Lemnos and abandoning her there, and likewise for abandoning Medea.

6. (p. 104) *I saw one with his head so foul with ordure . . . not clear if he were clerk or layman:* Dante is saying that this individual's head was so smeared with filth, it was impossible to tell whether or not he had the tonsure of a clergyman.

7. (p. 104) *Alessio Interminei:* A supporter of Dante's own party, the White Guelfs, in Lucca. It is not apparent what his specific crime was, but clearly, from the context, Dante is depicting him as having been guilty of betrayal.

8. (p. 105) *Thais:* Thais is the name of a number of courtesans at different points in history and in various works of literature. In this case, the name refers to the courtesan in Terence's play *Eunuchus*, written in the second century BCE.

CANTO XIX

1. (p. 106) *Simon Magus:* Simon Magus tried to buy the gift of healing from the apostles (hence the word "simony"—the sale of church offices).

2. (p. 108) *And he cried out . . . Boniface:* The speaker is Pope Nicholas III (pope from 1277 to 1280), who was notorious for simony and nepotism. Boniface is Pope Boniface VIII (pope from 1294 to 1303), who was pope during the year in which the poem is set, but dead by the time the poem

was written. So Pope Nicholas, here awaiting Boniface's arrival, mistakenly thinks the latter is dead already. From Dante's point of view, Boniface was one of the worst popes imaginable. Claiming universal supremacy over all secular powers in his bull Unam Sanctam of 1302, he instead destroyed the possibility of universal peace. And, in particular, he had meddled disastrously in Florentine affairs. Dante clearly took particular pleasure anticipating Boniface's fate, head down in a hole, his feet alight with flame.

3. (p. 108) *The beautiful Lady:* Personification of the church.

4. (p. 108) *I son of the She-bear:* Pope Nicholas was of the Orsini (meaning "little bears") family.

5. (p. 109) *a Pastor without law:* Pope Clement V (pope from 1305 to 1314), who came from France and transferred the seat of the papacy from Rome to Avignon.

6. (p. 109) *Jason . . . Maccabees:* Jason Maccabee bribed his way into the office of high priest.

7. (p. 110) *The Evangelist . . . ten horns received:* The images here are drawn from the Book of Revelation—written by Saint John the Evangelist—in which the whore of Babylon and the seven-headed Beast appear.

8. (p. 110) *Ah, Constantine:* The Roman emperor Constantine the Great (r. 306–337), who converted to Christianity and was supposed to have given a grant of land to the papacy—which became the Papal States—cutting a swathe across central Italy. For Dante, this started the rot, with the papacy becoming a secular power rather than a purely spiritual one. In the fifteenth century, the Donation of Constantine—the document that supposedly granted the land to the papacy—was proved to be a forgery.

CANTO XX

1. (p. 113) *Amphiaraus:* One of the Seven against Thebes. He had the dubious gift of foresight. Knowing he would die in battle, he hid rather than fight. But his wife gave him away, and the earth then swallowed him up. He plunged down into the Inferno as far as the judgment seat of Minos.

2. (p. 114) *Behold Tiresias . . . two entangled serpents:* In Greek mythology, Tiresias was a prophet from Thebes, who changed from man to woman upon striking a female serpent entangled with a male; he changed back after striking the male serpent.

3. (p. 114) *That Aruns is . . . Carrarese:* Aruns was an Etruscan soothsayer who supposedly foretold the civil war between Caesar and Pompey. He lived in the hills of Carrara (famous as the source of the finest marble), northwest of Florence.

4. (p. 114) *Manto:* Daughter of Tiresias, Manto was a sorceress and the legendary founder of Mantua, where Virgil was born. Over the next forty-five lines, Virgil describes, elegiacally, the geographical and early origins of Mantua, to counter any idea that sorcery infected the city during his own time.

5. (p. 116) *Eryphylus:* Eryphylus had prophetic powers and advised the Greeks of the propitious times to set sail during the Trojan War.
6. (p. 116) *Michael Scott:* Michael Scott (also spelled Scot) was a thirteenth-century Scottish philosopher, renowned as an expert in the magic arts.
7. (p. 116) *Behold Guido Bonatti, behold Asdente:* Guido Bonatti was an astrologer from Forlì, in northern Italy. Asdente, meaning "toothless," was the nickname of Benvenuto, a cobbler from Parma, who was well versed in astrology and, despite his illiteracy, knew the details of writings about how to foretell the future.

CANTO XXI

1. (p. 118) *the Arsenal:* The great shipyard of the Venetians. The showpiece of industry of its age, it was organized in "assembly-line" form, the galleys being fitted out progressively as they moved down the canal; this preceded Henry Ford's innovation in the early 1900s by centuries.
2. (p. 119) *Malebranche:* Meaning "evil claws," this is the collective name of the devils in the fifth ditch of the eighth circle.
3. (p. 119) *Saint Zita . . . barrators:* Saint Zita is the patron saint of Lucca, a city in Tuscany and a rival to Florence. In this passage, Dante shows his hostility toward the place, well furnished, as he says, with barrators—peddlers of corrupt and false lawsuits.
4. (p. 119) *Bonturo:* This reference to Bonturo Dati is heavily sarcastic, as he was renowned for corruption and, certainly in Dante's view, destined for Hell, though Dante could not feature him there as Bonturo was still alive in 1300 when the poem is set.
5. (p. 120) *the Santo Volto:* A miraculous crucifix brought to Lucca in the eighth century. It was supposedly carved by Nicodemus, a Pharisee who appears in the New Testament listening to Jesus' teaching. He fell asleep before finishing the crucifix and awoke to find it miraculously completed.
6. (p. 120) *the Serchio:* A river near Lucca.
7. (p. 121) *Malacoda:* Meaning "evil tail," this is the name of one of the devils.
8. (p. 122) *Alichino . . . Rubicante:* These names are all those of demons, which may well have been recognized by Dante's contemporaries from mystery play performances, or otherwise familiar as comic devils in popular culture.

CANTO XXII

1. (p. 124) *Vaunt-couriers:* An advance party; soldiers sent out in advance of the main army.
2. (p. 124) *Aretines:* People from Arezzo, a Tuscan city to the southeast of Florence.
3. (p. 126) *I in the kingdom of Navarre was born:* Identified by early commentators as Ciampolo (known also as Gian Polo), a retainer of King Thibault II

of Navarre (r. 1253–1270). Gian Polo was allegedly guilty of corruption, but no details are known.

4. (p. 127) *Friar Gomita:* A Sardinian guilty of corruption.

5. (p. 127) *Don Michel Zanche:* Another Sardinian guilty of corruption.

CANTO XXIII

1. (p. 130) *As go the Minor Friars:* In single file, in the manner of the Franciscan Friars Minor.

2. (p. 130) *Upon the fable of Æsop . . . the frog and mouse:* This refers to Aesop's fable about the frog who offers to carry a mouse, tied to its leg, across a stream. The frog then betrays the mouse by diving and drowning it. A passing bird of prey sees the dead mouse float to the surface and seizes it—along with the frog, which accordingly, gets its just desserts.

3. (p. 130) mo *and* issa: These two suffixes have the same meaning, indicating either a greater degree or superlative depending on the context.

4. (p. 132) *They had on mantles . . . for the monks are made:* The cowls of the monks at Cologne (sometimes read as "Cluny") were drawn down over their eyes.

5. (p. 132) *Frederick:* Emperor Frederick II had the reputation of weighing traitors down in lead and then boiling them—no doubt a useful reputation to have to deter treachery.

6. (p. 134) *Frati Gaudenti . . . taken by thy city:* Frati Gaudenti, meaning "jolly friars," refers to the Order of the Knights of Our Lady. Both Catalano dei Catalani and Loderingo degli Andalo were from Bologna, though Catalano was of the Guelf faction and Loderingo the Ghibelline. They had jointly been given the office of chief magistrate in Florence in 1266—to try to end faction fighting. This tactic failed, ending in riot, and Catalano and Loderingo were blamed as hypocrites working on behalf of their own interests.

7. (p. 134) *This transfixed one:* A reference to Caiaphas, the greatest hypocrite of all; he advised that Christ be given up to torture for the sake of the people, but in reality, he did this for his own political interest.

CANTO XXIV

1. (p. 136) *The husbandman . . . gleaming white:* The farmer (husbandman) running out of animal feed (forage) sees the open country (champaign) iced over and unyielding.

2. (p. 139) *For if Chelydri . . . with Amphisbæna:* The names listed here are those of legendary reptilian monsters in Libya; Dante is saying that the snakes he encounters here in this part of Hell are far more monstrous than those Libyan creatures.

3. (p. 140) *oppilation:* Obstruction or constraint.

4. (p. 140) *Vanni Fucci:* A notorious murderer from Pistoia, a city near Florence. He also, sacrilegiously, stole from the Sacristy of Pistoia and blamed another, which is a reason for his being here among thieves rather than among the violent in the seventh circle.

5. (p. 141) *Pistoia first of Neri . . . shall thereby be smitten:* Having been humiliated, Vanni Fucci seeks revenge by foretelling the defeat of the White Guelfs in Florence (an event that, in real life, led to Dante's exile from his native city). He couches his description in prophetic language—the Neri (Black Guelfs), having been driven from Pistoia, shall gather like a stormy vapor with their leader from the nearby Val di Magra and win a battle at Campo Picen, causing each Bianco (White Guelf) of Florence to be overcome.

CANTO XXV

1. (p. 142) *the figs:* An obscene gesture in which the thumb of each hand is placed between two fingers of that hand.

2. (p. 143) *Maremma:* A swampy area on the Tuscan coast.

3. (p. 143) *Cacus:* In Greek mythology, a giant, but here a centaur.

4. (p. 143) *By reason . . . Hercules:* Cacus stole Geryon's oxen, which Hercules was transporting as one of his twelve labors. Hercules caught up with him and bludgeoned him to death.

5. (p. 143) *Cianfa:* Cianfa dei Donati, who was a Florentine thief.

6. (p. 144) *Agnello:* Agnello dei Brunelleschi was another Florentine thief, with whom Cianfa (appearing as a serpent) here fuses.

7. (p. 145) *days canicular:* Dog days, or days under the Dog Star.

8. (p. 145) *in that part whereat is first received our aliment:* The navel.

9. (p. 145) *Lucan . . . Nassidius:* The classical Roman author Lucan described how the flesh of Sabellus, bitten by a snake, putrefied, and how Nassidius, likewise bitten, swelled and exploded inside his armor.

10. (p. 145) *Be silent Ovid, of Cadmus and Arethusa:* Ovid, the classical Roman poet, wrote of Cadmus' being transformed into a snake, because he slew a dragon that was sacred to Mars. Ovid also told of Arethusa, who while fleeing a river god, was changed into a fountain.

11. (p. 147) *Buoso:* Another Florentine thief.

12. (p. 147) *Puccio Sciancato:* Yet another of the Florentine thieves; however, he has escaped transformation.

13. (p. 147) *Gaville:* A Tuscan village, preyed upon by the last Florentine thief in this section, Francesco dei Cavalcanti. The villagers killed him, whereupon his kinsmen took vengeance on them for his death.

CANTO XXVI

1. (p. 148) *Prato:* A town ten miles northwest of Florence, Prato was another of that city's rivals.

2. (p. 148) *bourns:* Boundaries.

3. (p. 149) *Elijah's chariot:* Here, Dante is seeing deceitful sinners enveloped in flame, as Elisha saw the chariot of the prophet Elijah ascend in a cloud of fire.

4. (p. 150) *Eteocles with his brother:* Eteocles and his twin brother Polyneices were sons of Oedipus, whose quarrel over their inheritance ignited the war of the Seven against Thebes. They finally killed each other in single combat. As they burned on a pyre, the flames sprang apart because they hated each other so much.

5. (p. 150) *Ulysses and Diomed . . . gentle seed:* The Greeks Ulysses and Diomedes (spelled Diomed here), who fought in the Trojan War, were renowned for their deceit and cunning, as in the stratagem of the Trojan horse referred to in this passage. Following the defeat of Troy, a party of Trojans led by Aeneas fled, and his descendants went on to found Rome—thus, they were Rome's "gentle seed."

6. (p. 150) *Deidamia . . . borne:* Deidamia was abandoned by her lover, Achilles, when Ulysses and Diomedes persuaded him to join the war against Troy, even though they knew the prophecy of his death, which they concealed. The Palladium was the image of Athena in Troy, which was supposed to guarantee the city's safety and which Ulysses and Diomedes stole, as related in Virgil's *Aeneid.*

7. (p. 151) *From Circe . . . named it so:* On his way home from Troy, Ulysses and his men were held captive by the sorceress Circe. After they escaped, Gaeta (on the coast of Italy) was their first landfall. Gaeta had been given its name by Aeneas.

8. (p. 151) *Penelope:* The ever patient and faithful wife of Ulysses.

9. (p. 152) *Sardes:* Sardinia.

10. (p. 152) *Where Hercules his landmarks set as signals:* The Pillars of Hercules is the point at which Spain comes closest to Africa; from there, Ulysses and his ship left the Mediterranean, heading into the unknown of the vast ocean.

11. (p. 153) *Five times rekindled . . . underneath the moon:* Five lunar months, each approximately twenty-nine days.

CANTO XXVII

1. (p. 154) *the Sicilian bull:* A brass or bronze bull made by Perillus of Athens for Phalaris, the tyrant of Agrigento. Supposedly, a victim would be placed inside the bull, which was then heated, burning the victim inside, so that the cries of agony sounded like the bellowing of the bull. It has been said that Perillus himself was the first victim.

2. (p. 155) *My voice:* The speaker is Guido da Montefeltro (1223–1298), a faction leader in the central Italian region of the Romagna. He was known as "the Fox." Later in life, he repented his violent ways and became a Franciscan friar. But Pope Boniface VIII persuaded Guido to

assist him in outwitting his enemies by advising how to destroy their base, the city of Palestrina. The pope promised him absolution for the sin involved. Guido went along with the plan, but the absolution, in advance of the sin and without true repentance, was not valid and, at death, he found himself in the Inferno.

3. (p. 155) *the Romagnuols:* The people of the Romagna, in central Italy.

4. (p. 155) *The Eagle of Polenta . . . covers Cervia with her vans:* The Polenta family ruled Ravenna, and their symbol was an eagle. They extended their rule over the nearby city of Cervia.

5. (p. 155) *The city . . . Green Paws finds itself again:* The city is Forlì, in the northern portion of the Romagna. The French besieged Forlì but suffered heavy casualties in doing so. By 1300, Forlì was ruled by the Ordelaffi family, whose symbol, a lion, had green paws.

6. (p. 156) *Verrucchio's ancient Mastiff . . . wimbles of their teeth:* Malatesta da Verrucchio (the "ancient"), ruler of Rimini, and his son Malatestino ("the new") were thought of as mastiffs because of their ferocity. In 1295, they murdered their enemy Montagna. Their teeth are likened to "wimbles" (i.e., gimlets or drills).

7. (p. 155) *The cities of . . . white lair:* The Lamone is a river on which lies Faenza, and the Santerno is a river on which lies Imola. Both cities were governed at various times from 1275 onward by Maghinardo Pagano (d. 1302), whose symbol was the lioncel (a little lion)—as his power was slight—on a silver background, "the white lair."

8. (p. 156) *And that of which the Savio bathes the flank:* A reference to Cesena (one of the series of towns in the Romagna that Dante has been describing), through which the Savio River runs.

9. (p. 156) *Cordelier:* A man of the cord (i.e., a Franciscan friar).

10. (p. 156) *the High Priest:* Pope Boniface VIII.

11. (p. 157) *Constantine . . . Soracte:* The story goes that the Roman emperor Constantine the Great (r. 306–337) had been persecuting Christians but was then struck down by leprosy. He summoned Pope Sylvester (pope from 314 to 335) from his refuge at Mount Soracte. The pope cured him and, consequently, converted him to Christianity.

12. (p. 158) *Be not thy heart afraid . . . raze Palestrina to the ground:* Guido da Montefeltro is recounting Pope Boniface VIII's promise of absolution (see note 2 in this canto).

13. (p. 158) *one of the black Cherubim:* One of the fallen angels.

CANTO XXVIII

1. (p. 160) *Of Puglia . . . who errs not:* Puglia, here, refers to the southern part of Italy—a territory much larger than modern Puglia. Through the ages, this region saw great conflict, including the victory of Carthaginian general Hannibal over the Romans in 216 BCE at Cannae—that defeat of

the Romans was so great that there was a mound of gold rings gathered from the hands of the slaughtered Roman elite. Livy was the Roman historian who recorded this, and Dante rates him as a reliable source.

2. (p. 160) *Robert Guiscard:* Norman leader who took the region of Puglia from the Saracens in the eleventh century.

3. (p. 160) *Ceperano . . . Tagliacozzo:* Ceperana (here, Ceperano) was a pass taken by Charles of Anjou (1226–1285), who went on to defeat Manfred, son of Emperor Frederick II, at Benevento in 1266. Manfred's nephew Conradin was in turn defeated at Tagliacozzo in 1268.

4. (p. 161) *Ali:* Ali was the son-in-law of Muhammad, founder of Islam. Ali's claim to the caliphate was disputed, which led to the division between Sunni Muslims and Ali's followers, Shiites.

5. (p. 162) *Fra Dolcino . . . Novarese:* Fra Dolcino was the leader of a heretical sect, the Apostolic Brethren, against whom Pope Clement V ordered a crusade in 1305 (five years subsequent to this fictional warning from Muhammad). As a result, Fra Dolcino and his followers were starved out of their position in the hills near Novara, in northwestern Italy.

6. (p. 163) *Pier da Medicina . . . Marcabò:* Pier da Medicina was a troublemaker among the ruling families in the Po Valley, bounded by Vercelli and Marcabo.

7. (p. 163) *And make it known . . . of a tyrant fell:* Guido del Cassero and Angiolello da Carignano were two noblemen from Fano, who were drowned on their way to Cattolica in the early 1300s by Malatestino of Rimini, who had ambitions to take the territory of their home city.

8. (p. 163) *Between the isles of Cyprus and Majorca:* Meaning most of the Mediterranean.

9. (p. 163) *Argolic people:* The Greeks.

10. (p. 163) *Focara's:* Focara is the promontory near which the noblemen of Fano were drowned.

11. (p. 164) *Curio:* Curio urged Julius Caesar to cross the Rubicon (the river boundary of Rome's "home" territory in Italy), which provoked civil war in 49 BCE.

12. (p. 164) *Mosca:* Mosca dei Lamberti (see note 5 in canto 6).

13. (p. 164) *hauberk:* Armor—originally for the neck and shoulders.

14. (p. 165) *Bertram de Born:* Bertran de Born (spelled Bertram in Dante's text) was a French troubadour and political intriguer said to have stirred up rebellion by Prince Henry of England and Anjou—"the Young King" (li. 135)—against his father, King Henry II of England (r. 1154–1189).

15. (p. 165) *Achitophel . . . goadings:* Achitophel urged Absalom, son of the biblical king David, to rebel against his father.

CANTO XXIX

1. (p. 167) *Geri del Bello:* A cousin of Dante's father; he was murdered and, here, is resentful that no vengeance has been exacted on his behalf.

2. (p. 167) *Altaforte:* A stronghold of Bertran de Born, who appears in the previous canto.

3. (p. 168) *Valdichiana . . . Maremma and Sardinia:* The Valdichiana and the Maremma in Tuscany, and the lowlands of Sardinia, were particularly prone to malaria.

4. (p. 168) *Ægina:* An island (located near Athens), which the Roman goddess Juno afflicted with a terrible plague, killing all of its population except its king.

5. (p. 169) *currycomb:* A comb for grooming horses.

6. (p. 170) *I of Arezzo . . . had me burned:* The speaker is Griffolino. He was condemned to death around 1270 by Albert of Siena, who had used ecclesiastical connections to persecute him; Griffolino had claimed he could fly, so he was burned as a magician.

7. (p. 171) *Stricca . . . Niccolò . . . Caccia d'Ascian . . . Abbagliato:* In Siena, there was a select club of conspicuous consumers called the Brigata Spendereccia, or "Spendthrifts' Brigade." The four mentioned here were members: Stricca dei Salimbeni; Niccolò, possibly his brother; Caccianemico degli Scialenghi, who inherited lands in Asciano; and Bartolomeo dei Folcacchieri, known as Abbagliato, meaning "brain-addled."

8. (p. 171) *Capocchio's shade:* Known personally by Dante, Capocchio was an alchemist who was burned in Siena around 1293.

CANTO XXX

1. (p. 172) *Juno was enraged . . . drowned herself:* Jupiter had made love to the Theban princess, Semele, who then gave birth to Bacchus. This enraged Juno (Jupiter's wife), who got revenge, in part, by driving Athamas—Semele's brother-in-law—mad, to the point where he destroyed his own family as a result of his illusions, killing his son Learchus, which led Athamas' wife, Ino, to drown herself along with their other son.

2. (p. 173) *Hecuba . . . her mind distorted:* After being captured by the Greeks, Hecuba, wife to King Priam of Troy, saw both her daughter Polyxena and her son Polydorus dead. Driven out of her senses, she began to bark like a dog.

3. (p. 173) *the nefarious Myrrha:* The daughter of King Cinyras of Cyprus, who impersonated a lover of the king's in order to commit incest with him. Her life then threatened, she fled to Arabia and became a weeping myrrh tree.

4. (p. 173) *As he who goeth yonder . . . due form:* "He who goeth yonder" refers to Gianni Schicchi (mentioned by name in line 32 of this canto). This Florentine impersonated the dead Buoso Donati to get the will changed in favor of Buoso's son, Simone—and then cunningly arranged a legacy for himself. Dante's portrayal of Gianni Schicchi raving in Hell is harsher than the comic treatment that composer Giacomo Puccini (1858–1924) would later give him in the one-act opera *Gianni Schicchi.*

5. (p. 174) *dropsy . . . humors:* Dropsy is a condition in which the body swells with fluid, or "humors."

6. (p. 174) *Master Adam:* A counterfeiter who was burned in 1281. He had worked for the counts of Romena in the Casentino (here, Cassentin), in the upper Arno valley.

7. (p. 175) *The currency imprinted with the Baptist:* The florin, which carried the image of John the Baptist, Florence's patron saint.

8. (p. 175) *Guido . . . Alessandro . . . Branda's fount:* Guido, Alessandro, and their brother were members of the Romena family. Branda's fount refers to a spring near their castle.

9. (p. 175) *florins, which had three carats of impurity:* Florins that had twenty-one carats of gold instead of twenty-four.

10. (p. 175), *One the false woman is who accused Joseph:* Potiphar's wife, who, as told in the Old Testament, falsely accused Joseph of rape when he resisted her attempt to seduce him.

11. (p. 175) *Sinon, Greek of Troy:* Sinon was a Greek captive of the Trojans, who persuaded his captors, fatefully, to take the Trojan horse within their city walls.

12. (p. 176) *the horse:* The Trojan horse.

CANTO XXXI

1. (p. 178) *After the dolorous . . . Orlando sounded not:* Dante describes the noise he hears as being more terrible than that of the horn of Roland (here, Orlando), which sounded the alarm when Charlemagne's rear guard was ambushed and defeated at the Pass of Roncesvalles in the Pyrenees in 778 CE.

2. (p. 179) *Montereggione:* A fortified hilltop town near Siena. Its once-giant-like towers may still be seen, although somewhat reduced in stature.

3. (p. 180) *the pinecone of Saint Peter's:* A bronze monument—taller than any man—that once graced the courtyard of Old Saint Peter's Basilica.

4. (p. 180) *Three Frieslanders . . . thirty great palms:* The men of Friesland (in the modern Netherlands) were famed for their great height, but not even three, standing on one another's shoulders, could here reach up to touch the giant's hair. Given this, and the measurement of thirty palms from throat to navel, the giant stands more than fifty-two feet high.

5. (p. 180) *Raphael mai amech izabi almi:* Apart from the reference to the Archangel Raphael, these words have no obvious meaning. The speaker is Nimrod, the biblical mighty hunter, identified here as a giant and the builder of the Tower of Babel; he is condemned to speak an incomprehensible language, since the collapse of the Tower splintered one human language into many.

6. (p. 181) *gyre:* Turn.

7. (p. 181) *guerdon:* Reward.

8. (p. 181) *Ephialtes:* In mythology, Ephialtes was one of the giants who threatened to topple the gods by piling Mount Ossa on Olympus, and Mount Pelion on Ossa.

9. (p. 181) *Briareus:* In Greek mythology, Briareus was a giant with a hundred arms.

10. (p. 182) *Antæus:* Son of Poseidon (god of the sea) and Gaea (earth goddess), he was the greatest of wrestlers, and his tremendous strength came from contact with his mother earth. Hercules eventually overcame him by holding him aloft—so that his strength could not be renewed— and crushing him in a bear-hug.

11. (p. 182) *five ells:* An ell is a unit of measurement (no longer in use) equivalent to forty-five inches, so Antaeus is eighteen feet and nine inches tall.

12. (p. 182) *O thou . . . for thy prey:* Antaeus captured a thousand lions in the Libyan valley, where the Roman Scipio would later achieve final victory over Hannibal in the Battle of Zama in 202 BCE.

13. (p. 182) *Cocytus:* One of the great rivers of Hell, Cocytus forms the frozen lake at the base of the Inferno.

14. (p. 182) *Tityus . . . Typhæus:* More giants who challenged the gods and were defeated by them. Apollo and Artemis killed Tityus when he tried to rape their mother, Leto. Zeus killed Typhoeus with a thunderbolt while the giant was in the process of uprooting Mount Etna, beneath which he still lies smoldering.

15. (p. 183) *Carisenda:* Located in Bologna, this leaning tower (known also as Garisenda) sometimes looks as though it's falling when a cloud passes behind it.

CANTO XXXII

1. (p. 184) *stridulous:* Shrill, grating.

2. (p. 184) *Mamma and Babbo:* These first words, *Mamma* and *Babbo*, "mom" and "dad," signify the language one speaks from one's earliest years. Dante here is highlighting his boldness in writing in his native tongue, rather than using the more elevated Latin.

3. (p. 184) *those Ladies:* The Muses.

4. (p. 184) *Amphion:* Amphion played the lyre so beautifully that the stones of Mount Cithaeron came down to listen, arranging themselves as walls around Thebes. Dante hopes his own words will likewise move into place around the lowest pit of Hell.

5. (p. 185) *Tambernich . . . Pietrapana:* Tambernich is an unidentified mountain. Pietrapana probably refers to Petra Apuana in northwest Tuscany.

6. (p. 185) *two so close:* These are the brothers Napoleone and Alessandro degli Alberti, who politically opposed, quarreled over the estate of their dead father, the Count of Mangona, and killed each other.

7. (p. 186) *Bisenzio:* A tributary of the Arno River.

8. (p. 186) *and all Caïna . . . exonerate me:* As noted earlier, Caina is a region of Hell named after Cain, killer of his brother, Abel. Here are several individuals who murdered their own relatives. Mordred attacked and

mortally wounded Arthur, who was, in different versions of the story, either Mordred's father or uncle; Arthur then killed Mordred before he himself died. Focaccia dei Cancellieri of Pistoia murdered either his father or uncle. Sassol Mascheroni of Florence murdered a family member (it is unknown what relation) to get his hands on an inheritance. Camicion de' Pazzi of the Valdarno killed his relative Ubertino; in Hell, Camicion is awaiting the arrival of Carlino de' Pazzi, who he erroneously hopes will exonerate him (not only is Camicion's desire to be cleared of his crime futile, but so is his hope to encounter Carlino, as Carlino would end up in a different region Hell for his sin of betraying a White Guelf castle to the Black Guelfs).

9. (p. 187) *Antenora:* Named after the Trojan Antenor—who is said to have betrayed Troy to the Greeks—Antenora is the second region in the ninth circle.

10. (p. 188) *Bocca:* This is Bocca degli Abati, who was fighting on the Florentine Guelf side at the Battle of Montaperti in 1260. He was, however, a traitor, who sliced off the hand of the Guelf standard-bearer and brought down the standard, thereby creating chaos in the Guelf ranks and triggering their defeat.

11. (p. 188) *him of Duera:* A reference to Buoso da Duera. In the bitter contest between the invading Charles of Anjou and Manfred (r. 1258 1266)—heir to Emperor Frederick II's Italian possessions—Buoso was supposedly on Manfred's side. But Buoso betrayed him for a bribe and surrendered a pass near Parma, which he had been sent troops to defend.

12. (p. 188) *him of Beccaria:* Tesauro de' Beccheria, abbot of Vallombrosa and papal legate in Tuscany. Accused of plotting with the Ghibellines to bring them back to Florence, he was beheaded in 1258.

13. (p. 188) *Gianni del Soldanier . . . Ganellon . . . Tebaldello:* Gianni del Soldanier was a Florentine Ghibelline who switched sides in the rebellion, which led to the Ghibellines' defeat in Florence in 1258. Ganellon betrayed Charlemagne by giving away the route his army was taking through the Pyrenees, which led to the ambush of Roland and his rearguard troops at Roncesvalles. Tebaldello was a Ghibelline from Faenza who betrayed his city to the Guelfs of Bologna.

14. (p. 189) *Tydeus gnawed the temples of Menalippus in disdain:* Tydeus, king of Calydon, was one of the Seven against Thebes. He was fatally wounded by Menalippus, but before dying, he had Menalippus killed and decapitated, then tried to consume his head.

CANTO XXXIII

1. (p. 190) *Count Ugolino . . . Ruggieri the Archbishop:* Ugolino della Gherardesca was a Guelf leader in Pisa, who conspired with the Ghibelline archbishop Ruggieri Ubaldini to defeat a rival Guelf leader. The archbishop then saw

his chance to seize sole power and attacked Ugolino, imprisoning him with his two sons and two grandsons. In March 1289, the archbishop had the door to the tower where Ugolino and his family were incarcerated nailed up, and they were starved to death.

2. (p. 191) *mew:* A cage or coop.

3. (p. 191) *Gualandi with Sismondi and Lanfianchi:* Ghibelline families in Pisa.

4. (p. 193) *where the* Sì *doth sound:* Where the Italian language is spoken; *sì* is Italian for "yes."

5. (p. 193) *Capraia and Gorgona:* Pisan islands, just beyond the mouth of the Arno River.

6. (p. 194) *Friar Alberigo:* Friar Alberigo murdered his brother and nephew because of an insult, which he had pretended to forgive. He invited them to a feast and then had his servants kill them upon his signal, "Bring on the fruit!"

7. (p. 195) *Ptolomæa:* The third region of the ninth circle, where lie the murderers of guests—ultimate traitors to the sacred code of hospitality. It is named either after Ptolemy of Jericho, who murdered Simon Maccabee and two of Simon's sons at a banquet in the second century BCE, or possibly after Ptolemy XIII of Egypt, who brought about Pompey's death to curry favor with Caesar.

8. (p. 195) *Atropos:* The oldest of the three Fates, Atropos was known as the "inflexible" or "inevitable." She chose the means of death and ended the life of each mortal by cutting the life thread with her shears.

9. (p. 195) *Ser Branca d' Oria:* Branca d'Oria murdered his father-in-law, Michel Zanche, around 1290, so he could succeed him as governor of part of Sardinia. (We have already encountered Michel Zanche in the *Inferno,* boiling in pitch in the eighth circle for having been a swindler in life, guarded by the demons known as Malebranche.)

CANTO XXXIV

1. (p. 197) *Vexilla Regis prodeunt Inferni: Vexilla Regis prodeunt*—which translates to "the banners of the King go forth"—was a hymn from the sixth century; Virgil here changes it to "the banners of the King of the Inferno go forth."

2. (p. 198) *Dis:* Dante is using the name of the Roman god of the underworld for Satan.

3. (p. 198) *The Emperor of the kingdom dolorous:* Satan.

4. (p. 199) *Brutus . . . Cassius:* Brutus and Cassius, the assassins of Julius Caesar.

5. (p. 199) *night is reascending:* It is now the evening of Holy Saturday.

6. (p. 201) *the point to which things heavy draw from every side:* The center of the earth. This is the point at which up becomes down, and down becomes up.

7. (p. 201) *Judecca:* The fourth and final region of the ninth circle; it is named after the ultimate traitor, Judas Iscariot.

8. (p. 201) *And all the land* . . . : The Southern Hemisphere had no land until Satan and his cohorts fell into the core of the earth, displacing the material which then pushed upward to become the mountain that is Purgatory.

9. (p. 202) *Beelzebub:* Originally belonging to a pagan god, this name was taken over to refer to Satan.

BASED ON THE BOOK

1. Percy Bysshe Shelley, *The Major Works*, eds. Zachary Leader and Michael O'Neill (Oxford: Oxford University Press, 2003), 693.

2. George Gordon Byron, *Lord Byron: The Major Works*, ed. Jerome McGann (Oxford: Oxford World Classics, 2008) 768.

BASED ON THE BOOK

ALTHOUGH DANTE'S *COMEDY* IS REGARDED AS A FOUNDATIONAL TEXT IN Western literature, its reputation and influence has fluctuated, and while each part can only be fully understood as part of the whole project, it is the *Inferno* that has most consistently haunted the imagination over the last seven centuries. The early commentators worked to unlock the secrets of the great poem, and in turn, their work influenced other writers, as well as the artists who illustrated illuminated copies. In the fourteenth century, Giovanni Boccaccio was chief among them, toiling ceaselessly—while creating his own literary works such as *the Decameron*—to burnish the reputation of Dante whom he saw as his master, writing his biography and staging the first public lectures about Dante's work, which were paid for by the city of Florence. Through Boccaccio, Geoffrey Chaucer (ca. 1342/43–1400)—author of *The Canterbury Tales*—became familiar with Dante. Chaucer incorporated into that work the story of Ugolino (Hugelyn, as he became) in The Monk's Tale, while his poem *The House of Fame* (more than two thousand lines long) is almost a parody of Dante's work, quoting the *Inferno* and the rest of the *Comedy* extensively, but then veering off into anticlimax. Furthermore, in The Monk's Tale, Chaucer advises his audience to read Dante in full, word for word.

A century or more later, as those trends known collectively as the Renaissance emerged, Dante's influence fluctuated. The Italian scholar and poet Petrarch (1304–1374) became the master model for would-be poets, and Boccaccio that for prose writers, while humanists pursued first a refined classical Latin and then Greek, rather than the Italian Dante had forged into such great poetic material. However, Dante retained his iconic status for some. Leonardo Bruni (1370–1444), the great Florentine humanist, thought it worthwhile to write Dante's biography to prove that the poet's art was intimately connected with his active political life—the ideal of civic humanism—rather than being a withdrawal into contemplation, as Boccaccio had emphasized in his biography. And visual artists could find in Dante the most complete spiritual vision—evident, for instance, in the great scheme Sandro Botticelli (1445–1510) produced for illustrating *the Comedy*.

The refined Enlightenment of the mid-eighteenth century, parading a worldly skepticism of anything other-worldly or vulgarly gruesome, was a time during which Dante's reputation hit a low point. The art of the Romantics, however, brought new incarnations, and transformations, of Dante's image of the universe. They were particularly focused on the key stories of the *Inferno*—the doomed love of Paolo and Francesca; Ulysses and his determination to exceed mortal limits; and Ugolino, driven to his eternal gnawing of the head of Archbishop Ruggieri, who had brought about the starvation of Ugolino and his family by sealing them off in their prison tower. Dante's work affected the poets Samuel Taylor Coleridge (1772–1834), Lord Byron (1788–1824), and Percy Bysshe Shelley (1792–1822) immensely. For them, Dante was the heroic artist, unlocking the darkest secrets of the imagination. Shelley proclaimed that every word Dante wrote was "a burning atom of inextinguishable thought."[1] Dante's connection of the artistic with the political, and his defense of the mother tongue, fed into nationalist iconography. Byron produced his *Prophecy of Dante*, assuring his publisher that "Italy is on the eve of great things,"[2] meaning that Dante could help inspire Italian national renewal and unification.

As the neoclassical gave way to the Gothic style, Dante's reputation crested. Artists such as William Blake (1757–1827) and Henry Fuseli (1741–1825) had been inspired to produce illustrations of the *Comedy*, but it was the Pre-Raphaelite brotherhood that idolized him—in painting after painting, sketches, tapestries, and porcelain, as well as in poetry. They showed the salutary lessons of the *Inferno* and the idealized love for Beatrice—perfect for a Victorian society that sublimated, or just hid, sexuality. The parents of the painter Dante Gabriel Rossetti (1828–1882) paid homage to the poet by giving their son the name Dante, and he lived up to that name with the references to Dante's poetry in his art. Edward Coley Burne-Jones (1833–1898) took care that his engagement, and then his marriage day, marked the date of the death of Beatrice. Even William Gladstone (1809–1898), the grandest old man of Victorian politics, was a leading Dante scholar, who translated, among others, Dante's lines on Ugolino.

Each country had their Dante. The Americans first came to him through Ralph Waldo Emerson (1803–1882) and then, in the mid-nineteenth century, though Henry Wadsworth Longfellow (1807–1882), Charles Eliot Norton (1827–1908), and James Russell Lowell (1819–1891), who together founded the Dante Club at Harvard. It was Longfellow's translation, reproduced in this volume, that first brought Dante into an American idiom. France, later in the century and on into the twentieth, stamped its own tradition indelibly onto the visualization of Dante's texts, in the form of the illustrations by Gustave Doré (1832–1883)—which still spring to most minds when "seeing" the journey of Dante and Virgil)—as well as Auguste Rodin's (1840–1917) great project of Hell's gate, featuring at its apogee Dante as the Thinker.

The clarity of style and systematic thought that Dante presented was a powerfully attractive haven to modernist writers, given the uncertainties of twentieth century life and the drive of these writers to renew poetry as Dante had done in his own time. Ezra Pound (1885–1972) and T. S. Eliot (1888–1965) found him to be a secure foundation in their intellectual lives as they moved across the Atlantic and sought new roots in Europe. In Ireland, James Joyce (1882–1941), Samuel Beckett (1906–1989), and most recently, Seamus Heaney (b. 1939) looked to him as they, by turns, structured or tried to transcend the conflict arising from a society as divided as Florence around 1300. It is hard to envisage any full understanding of twentieth-century literature, at its most important and original, without also having an understanding of Dante.

The *Inferno* and the rest of the *Comedy* also live on in distinctively modern art forms, such as film. In 1911, Giuseppe de Liguoro made a silent film version of the *Inferno*, the first full-length feature made in Italy, achieving startling images with the limited special effects available then. Further cinematic forays into the underworld have brought together painting with film, as in the miniseries *A TV Dante* (1990) by filmmaker Peter Greenaway and artist Tom Phillips; there have been versions with animation and even, in 2006, a Claymation version by Alexis Waller, which makes particular sense of the transformation scenes of canto 25. A number of historical novels built around Dante's work have been published since the 1990s, including Matthew Pearl's *Dante Club*, which features Longfellow. In the hands of Romantic composers such as Franz Liszt (1811–1886) and Pyotr Ilyich Tchaikovsky (1840–1893), music was fashioned from Dante's work, and this musical response has moved readily into the world of rock, with homage to the master poet from bands such as Tangerine Dream, Joy Division, and of course, The Divine Comedy.

Dante sets out on his fateful journey again and again in drama, opera, and ballet. In 2010, at Sing Sing—the infamous jail in Ossining, New York—the inmates performed parts of the *Inferno* for a group of students, and then the students presented their own version. These performances ended with the same line, the last of the poem: "And then we emerged to look again at the stars" (note that this is not the same translation as presented in this book). In 2007, a rock-punk-jazz opera version of the *Comedy*—composed by Monsignor Marco Frisina, with lyrics cowritten and book by Gianmario Pay—opened in Rome. Unsurprisingly (though perhaps not so welcome among devotees) the *Inferno* has inspired a video game. The circles of Hell are a natural match for the levels of a game, and the strikingly visual, often gruesome, imagery fits neatly into the gamer's repertoire. The conversational mode Dante adopts in the original is not so natural to games—so he is translated into a crusader home from the wars, aiming to rescue Beatrice (who is presented as a sexual, rather than spiritual, ideal) from the underworld. Every time he overcomes a new sin, he "powers up." Following the release of the game there was a debate as to whether this was a desecration of a masterpiece or an avenue whereby a new generation could be made curious enough to engage with the original. Whether in sublime or occasionally ridiculous form, Dante's work appears poised to inspire new generations of readers and artists through the twenty-first century and beyond. And with digital resources—such as the Dartmouth Dante Project and similar university initiatives, as well as the multimedia iDante—there seem to be more and more opportunities to explore the complex universe as imagined by Dante.

FURTHER READING

ANDERSON, WILLIAM. *Dante the Maker.* New York: S4N Books, 2010.

BOCCACCIO, GIOVANNI. *Life of Dante.* London: Oneworld Classics, 2009.

BOYDE, PATRICK. *Perception and Passion in Dante's Comedy.* Cambridge: Cambridge University Press, 2006.

DORÉ, GUSTAVE. *The Doré Illustrations for Dante's "Divine Comedy."* Mineola, NY: Dover Publications, 1976.

ELIOT, T. S. *The Sacred Wood: Essays on Poetry and Criticism.* London: Methuen and Co., 1928.

ELSEN, ALBERT EDWARD. *"The Gates of Hell" by Auguste Rodin.* Stanford: Stanford University Press, 1985.

GALLAGHER, JOSEPH. *A Modern Reader's Guide to Dante's the "Divine Comedy."* Liguori, MO: Liguori Publications, 2000.

HAVELY, NICK. *Dante.* Oxford: Wiley-Blackwell, 2007.

HAWKINS, PETER. *Dante: A Brief History.* Oxford: Wiley-Blackwell, 2006.

HAWKINS, PETER S., AND JACOFF, RACHEL, EDS. *The Poets' Dante: Twentieth-Century Responses.* New York: Farrar, Straus and Giroux, 2002.

HOLLANDER, ROBERT. *Dante: A Life in Works.* New Haven: Yale University Press, 2001.

HOLMES, GEORGE. *Dante.* Past Masters. Oxford: Oxford University Press, 1983.

JACOFF, RACHEL, ED. *The Cambridge Companion to Dante.* Cambridge: Cambridge University Press, 2007.

LEWIS, R. W. B. *Dante: A Life.* New York: Penguin, 2009.

PEARL, MATTHEW. *The Dante Club: A Novel.* New York: Ballantine Books, 2006.

REYNOLDS, BARBARA. *Dante: The Poet, the Political Thinker, the Man.* London: I. B. Tauris & Co., 2006.

RUBIN, HARRIET. *Dante in Love: The World's Greatest Poem and How It Made History.* New York: Simon & Schuster, 2005.

SAYERS, DOROTHY L. *Introductory Papers on Dante.* Vol. 1, *The Poet Alive in His Writings.* Eugene, OR: Wipf & Stock Publishers, 2006.

VOSSLER, KARL. *Mediaeval Culture: An Introduction to Dante and His Times.* New York: Ungar, 1958.

WILSON, A. N. *Dante in Love.* London: Atlantic Books, 2011.